The Reading-Writing Workshop

STRATEGIES FOR THE COLLEGE CLASSROOM

Evelyn Hall

Donna Weyrich

Columbus State Community College

THE UNIVERSITY OF MICHIGAN PRESS

HR

ISBN-10: 0-472-03033-7
ISBN-13: 978-0-472-03033-0
Published in the United States of America
The University of Michigan Press
Manufactured in the United States of America

♾ Printed on acid-free paper

2009   2008   2007   2006   4   3   2   1

10|11|06

Acknowledgments

Authors need guardian angels, and Kelly Sippell, editor at the University of Michigan Press, has been ours. Kelly's boundless patience and support have made this book possible. Thank you, Kelly! We also wish to thank the University of Michigan Press staff for their diligent work on our manuscript. To our students and colleagues, we extend our sincere gratitude. Your contributions enabled us.

Grateful acknowledgment is made to the following authors, publishers, and individuals for permission to reprint personal or previously published materials.

Diane Bales for "Building Baby's Brain: Ten Myths" by Diane Bales. Reprinted with permission from the University of Georgia. Bales, D. (1998). *Building Baby's Brain: Ten Myths*. Athens, GA: University of Georgia, College of Family and Consumer Sciences.

Oktay Cini for responses to a questionnaire about past and present medicine in "Medical Professionals Talk about Past and Future Medicine."

Federal Trade Commission for "Ouch! Students Getting Stung Trying to Find $$$ for College," *http://www.ftc.gov/bcp/conline/pubs/alerts/ouchalrt.htm*.

Jan Fleck for postcard image of Ma'at.

Charlie Hall for drawing of "A Child's Perspective of Spring" by Joshua Hall.

John Heise for cuneiform writing, translation, and transliteration.

Renea Hushour for responses to a questionnaire about past and present medicine in "Medical Professionals Talk about Past and Future Medicine."

Barbara Ingham for "Antibacterial Soap a Waste of Time" by Barbara Ingham from *Food Science Newsletter*, January 2003, University of Wisconsin, Madison.

Knight-Ridder Tribune for "Fathers Provide Bridge over River of Goo" by Kathleen Parker. © *The Orlando Sentinel*, Aug. 16, 1998.

Tracy Liberatore for photo of Victorian storefront, 1914. Courtesy of Grandview Heights, Marble Cliff, Ohio Historical Society.

Library of Congress for photograph of Charles Darwin.

Jim and Tina Michaels for photographs of Jim and their child.

National Library of Medicine for picture of surgical instruments.

Sandra Porter for vocabulary journal and student marginalia.

The Soap and Detergent Association for "Antibacterial Products Provide Extra Protection against Germs," "FAQs about Antibacterial Soaps," "Overview," and "Some Facts about Germs and Disease," © The Soap and Detergent Association, Washington, DC, *http://www.cleaning101.com*.

Judith A. Westman for responses to a questionnaire about past and present medicine in "Medical Professionals Talk about Past and Future Medicine."

Every effort has been made to contact the copyright holders for permission to reprint borrowed material. We regret any oversights that may have occurred and will rectify them in future printings of this book.

Contents

To the Instructor   vii
To the Student   xiii

Chapter 1: To the Student: What's Important?   **1**
Introduction   2
Reading 1: Confessions of an ESL Teacher   3
Reading 2: Reading Well   15
Reading 3: Writing in Circles   21
    Writing Workshop: The Narrative Paragraph   28

Chapter 2: How Clean Should We Be?   **31**
Reading 1: Antibacterial Soap a Waste of Time   32
Reading 2: What the SDA Says about Antibacterial Products   38
    Writing Workshop: The Academic Essay and Paragraph   45

Chapter 3: To Tell the Truth and Nothing But   **53**
Reading 1: Ouch! Students Getting Stung Trying to Find $$$ for College   54
Reading 2: Academic Integrity   60
    Writing Workshop: Paragraph Support Using Concrete and Specific Details   67

Chapter 4: Young Minds   **76**
Reading 1: Building Baby's Brain: The Basics   77
Reading 2: Fathers Provide Bridge over the River of Goo   83
    Writing Workshop: Paragraph Unity   91

Chapter 5: Better Business for the Next Millennium   **94**
Reading 1: Mentofacturing: A Vision for American Industrial Excellence   95
Reading 2: Southwest Airlines' Rapid Climb   102
    Writing Workshop: Paragraph Coherence 1   108

Chapter 6: Science or Religion?   113
Reading 1: Kenneth Miller, Christian Evolutionist   114
Reading 2: Dyson Honored with Templeton Prize   119
Writing Workshop: Paragraph Coherence 2   125

Chapter 7: The New Medicines   131
Reading 1: Medical Professionals Talk about Past and Future Medicine   132
Reading 2: Fast Forward to 2020: What to Expect in Molecular Medicine   140
Writing Workshop: Concluding the Paragraph   146

Chapter 8: Artists' Perspectives of Spring   150
Reading 1: A Novelist's Perspective of Spring   151
Reading 2: A Poet's Perspective of Spring   155
Writing Workshop: Writing a Descriptive Paragraph   160

Appendix A: Vocabulary-Building Strategies and Sample Student Journal Entries   167
Appendix B: Sample Student Annotations   175
Index of Vocabulary from the Academic Word List   181

To the Instructor

The Reading-Writing Workshop: Strategies for the College Classroom is an integrated reading, writing, and critical-thinking skills text intended for college-bound ESL students at the intermediate to high-intermediate level. It was designed to be used in tandem with a solid grammar instruction component. The underpinnings of the text are derived from research, teaching experience, and convictions. These underpinnings have guided the design and organization of the text.

The Underpinnings

- *Students learn to read by reading and learn to write by writing.* Instructors and materials should immerse students in reading and writing experiences.

- *Reading and writing are related.* Students learn about writing by reading; students learn about reading by writing. Greater familiarity with language structure improves reading and writing. This connection should be reflected in instruction and materials.

- *Good writing is a product of engagement with ideas.* Students have plenty to say in their writing when given provocative starting points and opportunities to engage with serious ideas.

- *The paragraph is the foundation of college writing.* Premature introduction of the essay is a disservice to students. Extensive paragraph writing experience enables students to move easily to essay writing.

- *Writing and reading are both recursive activities.* Instruction in reading and writing should allow for the recursive nature of reading and writing.

- *Fluency in writing and grammatical correctness are not the same.* Initially, writing should focus on students' needs to write their thoughts and ideas. Organization and modification of content are parts of the revision process. Grammar correction is part of the editing process.

- *Vocabulary is a key component of reading ability.* Students want and need explicit vocabulary instruction and practice.

- *Dictionary use is an appropriate tool for vocabulary learning, particularly as a confirming technique.* Despite context clues being heralded as the preferred strategy by many ESL professionals and dictionary use being disparaged, second language learners have always, and will always, use dictionaries. As Keith S. Folse points out in *Vocabulary Myths* (2004), students carry their dictionaries with them, not their grammar books.[1] Students should be given the opportunity to learn about and use dictionaries along with context clues to improve reading.

- *Adult students can and should be put in the "driver's seat."* Students should examine their learning metacognitively and make decisions about what works best for them.

Reading Content

The reading selections represent various genres including journalism, poetry, fiction, and academic prose. Many are authentic; others have been adapted in order to place challenging subjects within reach of intermediate ESL students. The selections have been carefully chosen with several choices made as a result of student input. Sentence structure and the degree of embedding, not length of a reading selection, were the guiding factors for selecting at this level. The topics are serious and provocative so as to elicit critical thinking in both discussion and writing. Some themes—such as religion versus science or the season of spring—may initially seem less apt, but these topics have proven most successful in producing critical thinking. Student writing responses for these topics in particular have been among the best produced at this level—products of genuine engagement with ideas and the desire to be heard.

Vocabulary

Vocabulary study is both text-driven and student-driven. As a text-driven vocabulary program, vocabulary work targets the Academic Word List (AWL), the words most commonly found in academic texts (Coxhead 2000).[2] As a student-driven vocabulary program, vocabulary work requires each student to select additional unfamiliar words for study. This dual vocabulary identification process permits individualization of vocabulary work while better ensuring the study of words students will encounter in future college courses. Vocabulary work is prompted after the first quick reading of each selection in which students identify unfamiliar words and note the underlined AWL words. This timing provides students with the needed vocabulary

---

[1] Keith S. Folse, *Vocabulary Myths: Applying Second Language Research to Classroom Teaching* (Ann Arbor: University of Michigan Press, 2004).

[2] Averil Coxhead, "A New Academic Word List," *TESOL Quarterly* 34, no. 2 (2000): 213–38.

knowledge for their more careful second reading and is similar to the common recursive strategy many second language readers use as they go back and forth between reading and checking vocabulary to confirm meaning. Furthermore, students annotate AWL and other unfamiliar words in the space provided, reinforcing new vocabulary and making it readily available during the second more careful reading. Students are taught to maintain a vocabulary journal. The two most common strategies used by college students, use of context clues and use of the dictionary, are taught in Appendix A of the text. Students are asked to think about their vocabulary learning and make their own decisions about strategies for their vocabulary study and vocabulary journal work. After completing the text, students will have worked with 149 of the 352 AWL words found in the text plus many self-selected words.

Reading

Reading exercises target skills that are characteristic of successful college students. The skills practiced in this text include *activation of schema prior to reading, extracting main ideas, literal comprehension, margin notation, logical inference, application of information,* and *critical thinking.* The layout of the text permits annotation, a common learning aid used by college students and a means of encouraging active reading. After careful reading and annotating, students progress from literal to inferential, to critical and interpretative comprehension activities. Because these skill exercises are repeated for each reading selection in each chapter, students receive adequate practice to gain proficiency. In addition to skill development, reading as a recursive activity is highlighted as students return to the reading selection to revise their understanding and to further their engagement with the writer's ideas. The reader's engagement with the writer is a prelude to writing in two ways. First, as readers observe what others say about a topic, reading becomes a source for thinking and writing because it provides topics, ideas, information and, most significant, reactions from which to write. Second, noticing how others write serves as a model for student writers and as an excellent starting point for writing instruction.

Writing

As an integral part of each reading selection, writing is treated as a way for students to interact with texts and ideas, both as writers and readers. Writing is both a prelude and conclusion to each reading selection. Students keep a writing journal in which they write their responses to a question related to the reading selection before reading it. They review and add to their responses after a pre-reading discussion and again after completing the reading and accompanying exercises. This collection of ideas, based on pre-reading knowledge and new ideas gleaned from reading, becomes the basis of a paragraph written at the conclusion of each chapter.

In addition to highlighting the reader-writer connection, writing is also treated as a polished product. Because beginning students usually deal with sentence-level writing, this is likely to be the intermediate student's first encounter with paragraph work. Assuming this starting point, writing instruction focuses only on the paragraph. *The goal is a thorough understanding of the academic paragraph, which will form the foundation for essay writing beyond the intermediate level.* In each chapter, writing instruction focuses on an element of the paragraph. These elements include appearance, organization, development, unity, and coherence. The writing instruction includes explanations, references to the reading selections as models, and practice activities. Following writing instruction, a paragraph is developed from ideas collected in writing journals. Peer editing guidance emphasizes revision in tune with the writing focus of the chapter. Editing for mechanics is left up to the instructor, permitting the instructor to coordinate this work with concurrent grammar lessons.

The Format

The Reading-Writing Workshop: Strategies for the College Classroom is organized into eight thematic chapters. **Chapter 1, To the Student: What's Important?** leads students through the format of the text, provides instructions for the activities, and asks students to think about their learning. Chapters are organized to include

- Opening activities
- Reading selections with vocabulary and comprehension activities
- Writing instruction and writing assignments

Opening Activities

Chapters open with a picture, a quote, and several questions for discussion related to the theme of the chapter. The purpose is to activate students' thinking about the theme.

Reading Selections

Each reading selection includes:

- *In Your Writing Journal*
- *Before You Read...*
- *Step 1: Read for the Main Idea*
- *Step 2: Read for New Words*
- *Step 3: Read for Answers*
- *Step 4: Read between the Lines*
- *Step 5: Respond to the Reading*
- *Return to Your Writing Journal*

In Your Writing Journal

Before each reading, students write their response to a question related to the topic of the reading selection. They are encouraged to write as much as possible based on their own knowledge and experience.

Before You Read

In the first part of Before You Read, students discuss questions related to the topic of the reading selection. Questions promote students to share their knowledge, opinions, and experience related to the topic. The second part includes background information about the reading selection. Students then add new ideas to their writing journal response.

Step 1: Read for the Main Idea

Students read quickly and without stopping to discover a writer's main idea. Completion of a short outline asking for the main idea and a few supporting details follows. During this reading students mark unfamiliar words to work on in Step 2.

Step 2: Read for New Words

Students study AWL and self-selected unfamiliar words they will need for a more careful reading. Students interact with vocabulary in an ongoing vocabulary journal. In this step, glosses, which are simply vocabulary annotations, are added to the reading selection in the extra-wide margin, further reinforcing vocabulary learning. This is an important step because the more students do with new vocabulary, the more likely they will retain it.

Step 3: Read for Answers

Students do a more careful reading of the selection and answer literal comprehension questions. Annotations are added to the reading, again in the extra-wide margin. This is a way for the reader to interact with the writer, thus increasing comprehension.

Step 4: Read between the Lines

Students answer questions requiring them to understand implied meaning and understand the writer's attitudes.

Step 5: Respond to the Reading

Students are asked to think critically and respond to questions that require them to move beyond the reading selection.

Return to Your Writing Journal

Students review their response to the opening question and add their new ideas based on the reading selection.

Writing Instruction

Chapters conclude with a **Writing Workshop.** A paragraph-writing skill is presented, clarified with examples from the reading selections, and practiced using a variety of activities. Students then select ideas from their writing journal responses to develop as a polished paragraph. After writing a first draft, students work with a partner to revise their paragraphs. A list of questions provides a format for students to help each other. Student writers consider their partner's input and make final revisions before submitting their final copy.

Internet Activities

There are many appropriate websites complementing the reading topics. For example, students could go to the Center for Disease Control and Prevention to read about handwashing techniques while working on Chapter 2. Because Internet addresses change frequently, they have not been included. Teachers and students are encouraged to take advantage of Internet resources.

To the Student

Just as you cannot become a good soccer player or musician with only a few practices, you cannot become a good second language reader and writer without having many experiences with reading and writing. *The Reading-Writing Workshop* is designed to give you experiences with reading and writing in English. You will do a lot of writing, reading, and, of course, thinking. You will learn to write by writing and learn to read by reading. This book will also help you make connections—the connection between reading and writing and the connection between your ideas and the ideas of other writers. You will improve your writing by reading more. Reading shows you how other writers write, and reading gives you ideas for your own writing. Likewise, you can improve your reading by writing. The more you write, the more familiar you will become with structure and meaning in written English.

As you work through *The Reading-Writing Workshop*, you will understand how you are going to make connections between reading and writing. You will start by writing your own ideas about a topic. Then you will read the ideas of other writers and check your understanding by doing comprehension and vocabulary activities. Finally, after you are familiar with what other writers say about a topic, you will go back to your writing to add new ideas based on your reading. After completing the reading selections with writing, comprehension, and vocabulary work, you will focus on specific writing skills to apply to a paragraph based on the writing you have done earlier. **Chapter 1, To the Student: What's Important?** will show you how to do the activities in this book.

As you can see, you will be continually interacting with reading and writing in a back-and-forth process. The goal of all of this interaction is to develop strategies for using written English. Being an active learner is the key. We are offering you instruction and practice; you must be responsible for adding hard work and dedication.

Finally, you need confidence in yourself as you deal with your second language. Don't become discouraged by mistakes; learn from them. Making mistakes is part of learning to read and write a new language. Think of your learning as a garden that needs your care, and remember: sometimes you have to remove weeds to give the flowers room to grow.

1

To the Student: What's Important?

Ancient Cuneiform Writing

e-nu-ma e-lish la na-bu-ú shá-ma-mu

enüma elish lä nabû shamämü

Translation: When above heaven was not (yet) named

ca. 2800–2500 BCE (before the Christian era)

Source: http://saturn.sun.nl/~jheise/akkadian/Welcome_effects.html

Medical Advice

The Japanese eat very little fat and suffer fewer heart attacks than the British or Americans.

On the other hand, the French eat a lot of fat and suffer fewer heart attacks than the British or Americans.

The Japanese drink very little red wine and suffer fewer heart attacks than the British or Americans.

The Italians drink excessive amounts of red wine and suffer fewer heart attacks than the British or Americans.

Conclusion: Eat and drink what you like. **It's English that kills you.**

Source: yahoogroups.com, March 2002

Think about the Topic

- What do the contents of the two boxes have in common?

- Why do people need written communication?

- Can writers exist without readers?

- Are written and oral communication equally important?

- Make a guess about the meaning of this book's title, *The Reading-Writing Workshop: Strategies for the College Classroom.*

Introduction

The Reading-Writing Workshop: Strategies for the College Classroom is for ESL students who plan to enroll in U.S. college or university classes. Even when second language students have graduated from a first or native language university, they will need to adjust their reading and writing skills to fit U.S. college or university expectations. The focus of *The Reading-Writing Workshop* helps you prepare for academic reading and writing. You will work on understanding a writer's meaning and responding in your own writing. To help you understand the writer's meaning, you will also work on two common strategies for learning unfamiliar words. The wide variety of reading selections is an important feature of this book. The strategies that successful students use in their reading and writing assignments are another important feature. These three areas of focus—reading, writing, and vocabulary—will prepare you for the more advanced coursework you will do to get ready for other college or university classes.

Becoming Acquainted with This Textbook

Chapter 1 introduces you to ideas about reading, vocabulary, and writing and is different from the other chapters because it asks you to think about your own thinking and learning processes. Becoming more aware of your own learning processes will help you become a better learner.

Chapter 1 also describes the activities in the book. It looks a little different from the other chapters because it explains how to use the book. The About sections explain how to do the activities and exercises. The first time you come to an activity or exercise, you will find a gray About box above it. Pay careful attention to this information because you will do similar exercises and activities in each chapter.

An Overview of a Chapter

Each chapter opens with a picture, a quote, and some questions for discussion related to the topic of the chapter. Each chapter, except Chapter 1, includes two related readings.

Each reading selection in a chapter includes:

- a writing journal question
- pre-reading activities
- comprehension and vocabulary activities arranged in steps
- additional journal writing

Each chapter ends with a **Writing Workshop,** which includes writing instruction, practice activities, and a writing assignment.

Reading 1: Confessions of an ESL Teacher

In Your Writing Journal

About In Your Writing Journal

You will always do the *In Your Writing Journal* activity before you read each selection in a chapter. You will need a writing journal. This can be a spiral notebook or a section of a loose-leaf notebook.

Read the question and be sure you understand it. Write the question at the top of a new page in your writing journal. Write your response below it. Write as much as you can based on your own knowledge and experience. Focus on your thoughts and ideas, and do not worry about grammar or spelling errors for now. There are no right or wrong answers, so write freely.

You will add to your response after your pre-reading discussion and after completing the reading selection. You will not find specific answers to the question in the reading selection, but you will have new ideas to add to your journal response. You will also gain new ideas from your classmates.

Keep your writing journal in a safe place. Everything you write in it will be useful for your writing assignment in the *Writing Workshop* at the end of each chapter. You will find many ideas for your writing assignment in your writing journal. Many professional writers collect ideas this way.

Write this question at the top of a new page in your writing journal. Then write an answer based on your own knowledge and experience. Write as much as you can. Save your writing journal so you can add to it later.

How do you learn new words in a new language? Think about what works best for you.

Before You Read...

Discuss with Your Classmates

- Are you or any of your friends collectors? What kinds of things do you or your friends collect?
- Why do people collect things?
- Describe some unusual collections. Do you know anyone who collects words?
- What do you do when you come to an unfamiliar word in a text that is written in your first language? In a text that is written in your second language?
- What makes you remember a word?
- What does it mean to really know a word?

Consider This Background Information

- Unabridged dictionaries include all of the words for a language. Abridged dictionaries include only the most common words in a language.
- A lexicographer is a person who writes dictionaries.
- A logophile is a person who loves words.
- *The Complete Oxford Dictionary of the English Language* includes 20 volumes and costs more than $1,000.
- One hundred words make up about half of all written English.

- Second language learners worry about their lack of vocabulary more than any other aspect of their new language.[1]
- Good second language readers and writers have large vocabularies in their second language.[2]
- Educators have learned that the number of times a student encounters a new word is the most important factor in learning the word.[3]

Visit Your Writing Journal

What new ideas from your discussion can you add to your writing journal?

Step 1: Read for the Main Idea

About Step 1: Read for the Main Idea

Knowing the main idea of a reading selection is an important step to understanding it. Reading without stopping is a good strategy for discovering the main idea. Do not try to understand everything. Do not stop to find meanings for unfamiliar words, but underline them so you can work on them later.

These questions may help you think about the main idea:

- What is the topic of the reading selection?
- What is the most important idea the writer states about the topic?
- How can I state this idea in one sentence?
- What are a few supporting ideas that make the writer's main idea believable?

When you finish your quick reading, complete the short outline about the topic, the main idea, and a few supporting ideas that you remember from the reading. Your second reading of the selection will be a more careful reading.

Do not worry about the marginalia in Step 1.

---

[1]Keith S. Folse, *Vocabulary Myths: Applying Second Language Research to Classroom Teaching* (Ann Arbor: University of Michigan Press, 2004), 19–34, 130–31.

[2]Ibid, 25.

[3]Folse, Vocabulary Question (E-mail to Evelyn Hall, August 29, 2005).

First, read the selection quickly. Read it from beginning to end, and try to under-stand the writer's main idea and a few supporting ideas. Notice that some words for vocabulary study are underlined. Underline any other words that are unfamiliar to you. Don't stop reading to look them up. <u>Note</u>: *Do not underline the* **italicized** *words you see under the title of this reading selection. Complete the outline at the end of the selection.*

Confessions of an ESL Teacher

Disambiguate. Cacophony. Ubiquitous. Puerile.
Mendacious. Ambit. Esoteric. Beholden. Brio.
Spoonerisms. Egregious. Long Johns. Perchance.
Pugnacious. Ratchet. Pejorative. Unrequited.
Quixotic. Omnipotent. Omnipresent. Omniscient.
Lugubrious. Probity. Excoriate. Quintessential.
Caveat. Pontificate. Whence.

marginalia

I confess. I am a logophile. That means I am a word lover. The words above are from my word collection. I am a com-pulsive word collector. With all my hundreds of words, I must be a terrific ESL teacher.

Of course, word collecting is a good hobby for an ESL teacher, but there are other advantages.

First, word collecting is a very cheap hobby. Words are everywhere, and the collecting <u>process</u> <u>requires</u> only paper, pencil, and a dictionary. My words <u>reside</u> in special little note-books. Sometimes a word finds a home on a yellow sticky note, on the blank inside pages of books, or in the margins of the text. Housing my collection requires none of the fancy or expensive <u>equipment</u> other collections require.

Second, I get to decide what is collectible. I get to make decisions about which words are worth saving. I am attracted to some words because they are fun to say. Other words, such as *disambiguate,* have the perfect meaning for a thought or feeling that I was sure could not ever be described. *Disambiguate* is a verb, but it's not in the dictionary. It means to make something clear. It was formed from the adjective *ambiguous,* which describes something that is unclear or confusing. *Disambiguate* was coined (made up) by the Pentagon, the military department of the U.S. government. I bet a lot of ESL students want their teacher to disambiguate English grammar. Another one of my favorite words is *caveat.* It is on my list because I simply cannot remember its meaning. I have finally given in, and I have dog-eared that page of one of my dictionaries. These are only a few of the reasons for my word choices.

Finally, the most important advantage is a professional one. Shouldn't a logophile make a good ESL teacher? Word collecting is the perfect hobby for an ESL teacher. But here is my most embarrassing confession: *I really do not know how to teach vocabulary.* Maybe I can help students find ways to study new words, but really teach? I am guilty of having students match words and meanings, write definitions, identify related words, write sentences, fill in blanks, take words apart and put them back together, play word games, discuss meanings and uses, and countless other activities. Now, this list of activities makes me laugh. Even funnier is my final confession: I have forgotten the meanings of *many of the words* on the opening list just like many A+ students who have forgotten word meanings after a vocabulary test. How can this be possible?

I can only conclude that there must be many secrets to second language vocabulary learning. In this chapter, you will begin working on unfamiliar words, and most important, the activities that depend on words—reading and writing. Maybe, you can solve the mystery of learning second language vocabulary.

Based on your first reading, complete this outline:

The topic: _____
                            Write a word or phrase.

The main idea: _____
                            Write a sentence. Choose from a, b, or c.

                            _____

Choose the sentence that best states the main idea, and write it down. Remember to think about the entire reading selection.

   a. This ESL teacher confesses that she has tried many different activities to help students learn new vocabulary, but she still isn't sure how to teach vocabulary.

   b. Good ESL teachers usually have hobbies that involve words.

   c. Word collecting is a convenient hobby, but it may not help ESL teachers teach vocabulary.

Some supporting ideas: *need only paper, pencil, and a dictionary*_____
                          Write a different phrase or sentence on each line.

                          *Word collecting didn't help this teacher.*_____

Do the supporting ideas help prove the main idea?

Step 2: Read for New Words

About Step 2: Read for New Words

Before you reread a selection for a more thorough understanding in Step 3, you need to understand unfamiliar words. You will study words from the reading selection that are on the **Academic Word List (AWL).** The words on this list are important because they are in many academic textbooks. You will also work on the unfamiliar words that you underlined during your first reading of the selection.

Selecting Words for Study

Did you underline *logophile* as an unfamiliar word to learn? This word is an example of a **passive** vocabulary word. Passive vocabulary includes words that you recognize and understand while reading and listening, but you do not usually use them while writing and speaking. These are also words that you will see but that you may not need to study because you don't use them frequently. **Active** vocabulary includes all the words that you are able to use and use correctly. For example, *logophile* is a word for which you do not need to learn the exact meaning because you probably will not use this word in your speaking and writing after you complete this reading selection, although you might call someone a "word lover." It's good enough in this case to recognize the word when you see it in context. Because your goal is to increase your active vocabulary, you should make frequently used words and the AWL words part of your active vocabulary. If you are unsure about including a word in your vocabulary journal, your instructor can help you decide.

Practicing Vocabulary-Building Strategies

To learn and practice vocabulary-building strategies, take the time to study Appendix A and do the exercises provided. After each reading in the text, you will be prompted to return to this appendix to refresh your memory of these strategies and to sharpen your skills. These vocabulary-building strategies will make it possible for you to successfully complete your vocabulary journal. These strategies will also help you acquire many new words that will be valuable to you when you complete reading and writing tasks in other college courses.

Starting Your Vocabulary Journal

The best way to learn new words is to interact with them. Simply reading a new word or even looking up its definition in the dictionary will not add the word to your active vocabulary. To make the new words your own, follow these steps to complete your vocabulary journal:

First, write each underlined word (the AWL words and the words that you have underlined) in your vocabulary journal. Copy the sentence in which you found the word. Copying the sentence is important because the sentence provides clues to the word's meaning. It will also give you an example of the correct usage of the word. It is important to work with an unfamiliar word in a sentence.

Second, decide what part of speech the word should be, based on its place in the sentence, and note this in your vocabulary journal.

Third, guess the meaning of each word as it is used in the sentence. Consider the meaning of the whole sentence and the main idea of the entire reading.

Fourth, confirm your guess by looking the word up in your translation and ESL dictionaries. Discuss the word's meaning with your classmates and instructor. Add to your vocabulary journal any notes that will help you remember the meaning of the word and prepare you to use it correctly in your own speech and writing.

Fifth, write your own sentence using the word. Now you have made the new word *your* new word, a part of your active vocabulary.

Sixth, gloss the reading selection, which means returning to the reading and adding notes in the wide margin next to the text. These notes are called glosses. They are similar to the glossaries at the end of textbooks because they provide word meanings. While glossing the reading selection, you are studying new vocabulary. Also, after glossing, you will have vocabulary information available the next time you read the selection, so it will be easier to comprehend the reading.

AWL Words to Know

These AWL words in order of appearance are underlined in the reading selection. Add them to your vocabulary journal.

process	reside	ambiguous	professional	identify
require	equipment	military	definition	conclude

Next, add any unfamiliar words that you underlined in Reading 1.

Follow these steps to complete your vocabulary journal:

1. Write the word and the sentence in the reading containing the word.
2. Note what part of speech the word should be based on its place in the sentence.
3. Guess the meaning of the word based on the sentence's meaning and the main idea of the reading selection.
4. Discuss your guess with your instructor and classmates, and confirm your guess by looking the word up in the dictionary. Add any notes that will help you remember the meaning of the word.
5. Use the word in your own original sentence.
6. Gloss the reading selection before reading it a second time.

Step 3: Read for Answers

About Step 3: Read for Answers

By now you have an idea of the writer's main idea, and you have studied vocabulary words that you need for a more complete understanding. In this step, you will reread the selection carefully and add **marginalia** or special notes in the wide margin on the right side of the reading selection. Adding notes is a special way for the reader to become involved with the writer. (You will learn about marginalia in Reading 2 of this chapter.) Answers to these questions can be found in the reading selection; you may need to return to it to find the answers.

Reread Reading 1. Then return to the reading to find the information that you need to complete this exercise. Prepare to discuss your answers.

1. What is a *logophile*?

2. List three advantages of word collecting as a hobby. Write an example for each.

Advantage	Example
a. *It's a cheap hobby.*	*You only need paper, a pencil, and a dictionary.*
b.	
c.	

3. The writer says the most important advantage of word collecting is a professional one. However, this advantage turns out to be a disadvantage. Why?

4. The writer makes a confession about teaching vocabulary. What is it?

Step 4: Read between the Lines

About Step 4: Read between the Lines

You will not find answers to these questions in the reading selection, but it is still possible to answer them. Meaning that is not stated directly is called **implied meaning**. Based on the information the writer gives, you can understand implied meaning. When you do this, you are **making inferences.** This is an important reading skill. After your careful reading, your understanding should be greater, and you will be able to make inferences about the writer's feelings and attitudes.

Do you think the writer of Reading 1 would agree or disagree with these statements? Return to the reading to discover the writer's opinion, and then circle A for agree or D for disagree. Prepare to give reasons for your answers. Remember to think about the <u>writer's opinion</u>, not your own opinion.

<u>Example</u>

Sometimes it's acceptable for people to use words that aren't   Ⓐ   D
in the dictionary.

The answer is A for agree.

In the sentences that follow, the writer gives an example of a word that is not in the dictionary. The writer explains that *disambiguate* was made up and used by the U.S. government.

> *Disambiguate* is a verb, but it's not in the dictionary. It means to make something clear. It was formed from the adjective, <u>*ambiguous*</u>, which describes something that is unclear or confusing. *Disambiguate* was coined (made up) by the Pentagon, the <u>military</u> department of the U.S. government.

1. Word collectors make good ESL teachers.   A   D

2. There are many ways to practice L2 vocabulary words.   A   D

3. ESL students often learn new vocabulary without classroom instruction.   A   D

4. A good ESL teacher knows the best way to teach vocabulary.   A   D

5. It's hard for a teacher to know which activities will help students.   A   D

Step 5: Respond to the Reading

About Step 5: Respond to the Reading

Now it is time for you to join the discussion. Think about the information the writer has presented and your understanding of his or her attitude or opinion about the topic. Before answering these questions, think about your ideas and opinions about the topic. Express your own thoughts and opinions about the topic when you answer the questions in this step.

Reflect on your own knowledge and experience, and answer the questions. Remember to think about your own opinions. Be ready to discuss your answers.

1. The writer does not solve the problem of how to teach vocabulary. List some suggestions for teaching new vocabulary.

2. Would you expect to have a successful learning experience in this teacher's class? Why or why not?

Return to Your Writing Journal

Return to your writing journal, and review your response to the opening question for Reading 1. What new ideas and opinions do you have now? Have your teachers asked you to do some of the activities mentioned in the reading selection? Did these activities help you? Have you ever earned an A on a vocabulary test and then forgotten the meanings of the words on the test? Why do you think this happens? What do you think teachers can do to help students learn vocabulary? Add your new thoughts to your response. Write as much as you can.

Reading 2: Reading Well

In Your Writing Journal

Write this question at the top of a new page in your writing journal. Then write an answer based on your own knowledge and experience. Write as much as you can. Save your writing journal so you can add to it later.

How did you learn to read and write in your first language?

Before You Read...

Discuss with Your Classmates

- Why is it important for children to learn to read?
- Why do you think young children pretend to read and write?
- How is academic reading different from pleasure reading?
- Make a guess about the meaning of this quote from W. S. Landor, a British author: "What is reading but silent conversation."
- Think of all the different things other than books, newspapers, and magazines that you read in a day. Which are necessary? Which are for pleasure?
- How would your life be different if you could not read even a single word?

Consider This Background Information

- Most children learn to read when they are six or seven years old.
- Children as young as three can distinguish writing in their native language from writing of other languages.
- Adults who are better-than-average readers are also more likely to have higher-paying jobs.
- UNESCO (The United Nations Educational, Scientific, and Cultural Organization) reports that there are an estimated 862 million illiterate adults in the world, about two-thirds of whom are women.
- The most literate (percentage of the population that is able to read and write) country in the world is not the United States. According to the *CIA World Factbook* for 2005, Vatican City, Norway, Australia, Liechtenstein, Luxemburg, Denmark, Findland, and Georgia all have a literacy rate of 100 percent.

- Arthur Krystal, a *New York Times* writer, reported that if you were to read 135 books a day every day, for a year, you wouldn't finish all of the books published in one year in the United States.

Visit Your Writing Journal

What new ideas from your discussion can you add to your writing journal?

Step 1: Read for the Main Idea

First, read the selection quickly. Read it from beginning to end, and try to understand the writer's main idea and a few supporting ideas. Notice that some AWL words for vocabulary study are underlined. Underline any other words that are unfamiliar to you. Don't stop reading to look them up. Complete the outline at the end of the selection.

Reading Well

marginalia

To read well, readers must be active—never <u>passive</u>. Reading may seem like a passive activity, but it requires serious attention in order to understand a writer's message. The same kind of <u>interaction</u> that connects speaker and listener must <u>occur</u> between writer and reader, but with one big difference—the writer has only one chance to offer his or her ideas and thoughts. However, the reader has many chances to understand them. The reader can return to a reading selection again and again. *Active reading requires <u>revision</u>* or changes in the same way that writing requires revision. Like the first copy or <u>draft</u> of a composition, the first reading is only a starting place.

As an academic reader, you must find ways to understand the writer's message. After your first quick non-stop reading, it's time to dig deeper into the reading selection.

This is where the action starts. Throw away your favorite yellow highlighter. (I know this sounds a little crazy.) It is a passive learning tool. It's too easy to read and mark and mark and mark and mark. Before long, you've got a page that's mostly yellow, right? To read with real understanding, you must become <u>involved</u> with the writer. Successful academic readers read with a pencil in hand. They are ready to <u>respond</u> and question the writer. They write notes in the margins of their reading selections. Such notes are called *margin annotations* or *marginalia*. These are brief comments, questions, reactions, drawings, stars, or anything that is helpful. Schoolteachers know this habit as "book abuse" because it shouldn't be done in books you don't own. Librarians think of themselves as the "book police" and fine people who write margin notes for their "crimes." Good students (who have their own books) know this as a valuable learning <u>strategy</u>.

Marginalia are personalized tools, so you do not have to write in a way that others can read and understand. You are creating a personal learning tool.

The margins are a good place for:

■ questioning the writer's views and <u>sources</u>
■ agreeing or disagreeing with the writer
■ marking key <u>concepts</u> to remember
■ marking key concepts to clarify
■ marking ideas to use in writing or discussion
■ making connections to other information you have or other things you've read

Look at the examples of marginalia in Appendix B. What kinds of things are marked in these student examples?

Steps 3–5 of the reading selections require careful reading and rereading. Add marginalia as you do your careful reading. Continue to go through the reading selection, trying to understand more each time you read it. Your annotated text will be useful for class discussions, so mark any parts that you need to ask about during class discussions.

This is the way successful academic readers read after they have discovered the main idea. <u>Remember</u>: The more involved you are with the writer and the writing, the more you will understand and remember. Then you will have more to say in your writing.

Based on your first reading, complete this outline:

The topic: _____

                     Write a word or phrase.

The main idea: _____

                     Write a sentence. Choose from a, b, or c.

                     _____

Choose the sentence that best states the main idea, and write it down. Remember to think about the entire reading selection.

    a. Good readers write notes in their textbooks.

    b. Good readers should use the same kinds of marginalia so it is easy for others to understand.

    c. Good readers become involved with the writer and the reading selection.

Some supporting ideas: *read again to revise understanding*

                     Write a different phrase or sentence on each line.

                     add my own marginalia

                     _____

Do the supporting ideas help prove the main idea?

Step 2: Read for New Words

Return to Appendix A to review vocabulary-building strategies.

AWL Words to Know

These AWL words are underlined in order of appearance in the reading selection. Add them to your vocabulary journal.

passive	occur	draft	respond	sources
interaction	revision	involved	strategy	concepts

Next, add any unfamiliar words that you underlined in Reading 2.

Follow these steps to complete your vocabulary journal:

1. Write the word and the sentence in the reading containing the word.

2. Note what part of speech the word should be based on its place in the sentence.

3. Guess the meaning of the word based on the sentence's meaning and the main idea of the reading selection.

4. Discuss your guess with your instructor and classmates, and confirm your guess by looking up the word in the dictionary. Add any notes that will help you remember the meaning of the word.

5. Use the word in your own original sentence.

6. Gloss the reading selection before reading it a second time.

Step 3: Read for Answers

Reread Reading 2, and add marginalia in the wide right-hand margin. Then return to the reading to find the information that you need to complete this exercise. Prepare to discuss your answers.

1. What are some characteristics of a good reader?

2. What strategy is suggested for becoming engaged in a reading assignment?

3. What are margin annotations or *marginalia*?

4. List three different kinds of marginalia.

   a.

   b.

   c.

5. Why does the writer recommend <u>not</u> using a highlighter?

6. What does this statement mean: "Reading requires revision"?

Step 4: Read between the Lines

Do you think the writer of Reading 2 would agree or disagree with these statements? Return to the reading to discover the writer's opinion, and then circle A for agree or D for disagree. Prepare to give reasons for your answers. Remember to think about the <u>writer's opinion</u>, not your own opinion.

1. Receiving information is less work than giving information.   A   D

2. If you own your textbooks, it's a good idea to write in them.   A   D

3. Instructors should tell students how to mark in their books.   A   D

4. College students should keep their books clean so they can resell them for more money.   A   D

Step 5: Respond to the Reading

Reflect on your own knowledge and experience, and answer the questions. Remember to think about <u>your own opinions</u>. Be ready to discuss your answers.

1. In the early stages of writing this book, "Reading Well" was entitled "How to Adopt a Book." What is your opinion of the second title? If you were naming Reading 2, which title would you select? Why? Can you think of any other titles that might be appropriate?

2. How could marginalia be used in nonacademic reading material? Give some examples.

3. Many people disagree with the author's statement, "Throw away your favorite yellow highlighter." The authors seem to be afraid that students will *get carried away* with highlighting. What is your opinion?

4. Apply the writer's suggestions by adding glosses and marginalia to this paragraph.

marginalia

Good students have always known the value of marginalia. In fact, Erasmus, a Dutch writer and teacher who lived from 1466 to 1536, told his students to write in their books; otherwise, they would never learn. Medieval students trying to read Latin texts added notes as they read.

marginalia

In the early 1900s, British school children learned how to write "good margin annotations." Pierre de Fermat, a great seventeenth century mathematician, wrote in a margin: "I have discovered a truly remarkable proof (solution to a math problem) but this margin is too small to contain it." To this day, no one has found his proof or determined whether this was only a scholarly joke. Today, successful academic readers continue to depend on marginalia to increase their reading comprehension.

Return to Your Writing Journal

Return to your writing journal, and review your response to the opening question for Reading 2. What new ideas and opinions do you have now? Has reading this selection helped you remember some other ideas about your early experiences with reading and writing? Do you have some new ideas about reading? Add your new thoughts to your response. Write as much as you can.

Reading 3: Writing in Circles

In Your Writing Journal

Write this question at the top of a new page in your writing journal. Then write an answer based on your own knowledge and experience. Write as much as you can. Save your writing journal so you can add to it later.

How do you go about writing a composition in English?

Before You Read...

Discuss with Classmates

- What kinds of writing have you done in your first language? In English?
- What steps do you follow when you write?
- What are the characteristics of a good writer?
- Are there any special things you do to get started on a writing assignment?
- Do you wait until the last minute to do a writing assignment?
- Speculate about the meaning of the title of the reading selection, "Writing in Circles."

Consider This Background Information

Here is what some published writers have said about their writing:

- "Once you can express yourself, you can tell the world what you want from it. . . . All changes in the world, for good or for evil, were brought about by words." Jacqueline Kennedy Onassis
- "Writing is hard work. A clear sentence is no accident. Very few sentences come out right the first time. Remember this in moments of despair. If you find that writing is hard, it's because it *is* hard." William Zinsser
- "You write in order to read what you've written and see if it's O.K. and, since of course it never is, to rewrite it—once, twice, as many times as it takes to get it to be something you can bear to reread." Susan Sontag
- "Then comes the warm part: when you already have something to work with, upgrade, edit." Susan Sontag
- "My method is one of continuous revision. While writing a long novel, every day I loop back to earlier sections to rewrite. . . ." Joyce Carol Oates
- "I know you believe you understand what you think I said [wrote] but I am not sure you realize that what you heard [read] is not what I meant." Anonymous

Visit Your Writing Journal

What new ideas from your discussion can you add to your writing journal?

Step 1: Read for the Main Ideas

First, read the selection quickly. Read it from beginning to end, and try to understand the writer's main idea and a few supporting ideas. Notice that some AWL words for vocabulary study are underlined. Underline any other words that are unfamiliar to you. Don't stop reading to look them up. Complete the outline at the end of the selection.

Writing in Circles

marginalia

As a college student, you will have to show your understanding of various subjects by writing. The writing work in this book will help prepare you for this <u>task</u>.

Many first and second language writing teachers teach writing as a process that can be divided into separate steps: pre-writing, drafting, revising, and editing. Each step has a purpose.

Step	Purpose
pre-writing	to choose a topic, gather and sort ideas, and decide the treatment of the topic
<u>drafting</u>	to write your ideas
<u>revising</u>	to <u>evaluate</u> your written ideas and improve them
<u>editing</u>	to correct mechanical <u>errors</u> (usage, grammar, spelling, etc.)

Some writers move from one step to the next. They complete each step before moving to the next step. This is referred to as a *linear writing process*. Many writers like the feeling of organization that comes from working through the steps.

Other writers switch back and forth between the steps. This is referred to as a *recursive writing process*. This <u>style</u> of writing is more like the way many people think. There are always thoughts entering our minds.

In recursive writing, the same steps of writing are used, but they are *not always used in linear order*. The writing process is considered nonlinear. In other words, you don't have to complete one step before moving on to the next, and you can return to any step at any time. You might do some revising or editing while you are still drafting. You might add an idea that was not in your prewriting. You might even return to a reading selection or your writing journal. It's even OK to change your topic sentence.

Many writers are more comfortable with recursive writing. Lots of writers use a recursive writing method without even knowing it. Recursive writers know that revising is the key to saying what they mean. Remember Susan Sontag's <u>quote</u>? "Then comes the warm part: when you already have something to work with, upgrade, edit." As a novice second language writer, practice the recursive method of writing. Go back and forth between writing steps; do all of those *re-* activities—*reread, revise, rewrite, return to a classmate for discussion,* and *resubmit* your <u>drafts</u> to your teacher. The writing tasks in this text will help you discover the rewards of the recursive writing process. Remember, a better process yields a better product.

Based on your first reading of the selection, complete this outline:

The topic: _____
                                    Write a word or phrase.

The main idea: <u>Linear and recursive writing are</u>_____
                                    Complete the sentence.

                                    _____

Some supporting ideas: <u>same activities for both</u>_____
                                    Write a different phrase or sentence on each line.

                                    _____

                                    _____

Do the supporting ideas help prove the main idea?

Step 2: Read for New Words

Return to Appendix A to review vocabulary-building strategies.

AWL Words to Know

These AWL words in order of appearance are underlined in the reading selection. Add them to your vocabulary journal.

task	evaluate	style
drafting	editing	quote
revising	errors	drafts

Next, add any unfamiliar words that you have underlined in Reading 3.

Follow these steps to complete your vocabulary journal:

1. Write the word and the sentence in the reading containing the word.

2. Note what part of speech the word should be based on its place in the sentence.

3. Guess the meaning of the word based on the sentence's meaning and the main idea of the reading selection.

4. Discuss your guess with your instructor and classmates, and confirm your guess by looking up the word in the dictionary. Add any notes that will help you remember the meaning of the word.

5. Use the word in your own original sentence.

6. Gloss the reading selection before reading it a second time.

Step 3: Read for Answers

Reread Reading 3, and add marginalia in the wide right-hand margin. Then return to the reading to find the information that you need to complete this exercise. Prepare to discuss your answers.

1. What are the steps of writing processes?

    a.

    b.

    c.

    d.

2. How are writing as a linear process and writing as a recursive process different?

3. What is the difference between revising and editing?

Step 4: Read between the Lines

*Some statements and questions that writing instructors might say follow. If you think the instructor is teaching writing as a **linear** process, write **L**. If you think the instructor is teaching writing as a **recursive** process, write **R**. Prepare to give reasons for your answers.*

_____ 1. "Your writing shows that you have included all of the details that were listed in your pre-writing activities."

_____ 2. "I see that you have included some interesting ideas that you hadn't thought of when you did your pre-writing."

_____ 3. "Your paragraph would be a lot better if you knew exactly what you wanted to say before you started writing."

_____ 4. "Now that you have finished revising, please start editing your paragraph."

_____ 5. "All the rereading you did really helped you choose some great details."

_____ 6. "I'm having a hard time following all of your lines and arrows, but I think you really know what you want to say to the reader."

Step 5: Respond to the Reading

Reflect on your own knowledge and experience, and answer the questions. Remember to think about <u>your own opinions</u>. Be ready to discuss your answers.

1. How long does it take to write a good paragraph? Explain your answer.

2. Doing a writing assignment the night before it is due can cause problems—especially for recursive writers. What kinds of problems?

3. After reading the selection, what does the title "Writing in Circles" mean to you?

Return to Your Writing Journal

Return to your writing journal, and review your response to the opening question for Reading 3. What new ideas and opinions do you have now? Which writing method have you used in the past? Which writing method do you prefer after reading this selection? Add your new thoughts to your response. Write as much as you can.

About Writing Workshop

Each chapter ends with a **Writing Workshop.** You will learn and practice specific writing skills. You will review and sort though all of your journal writing and write a composition. During the writing sessions you will have time to interact with classmates and your instructor. You will need your journals and reading materials so you can refer to them often for ideas.

Writing Workshop: The Narrative Paragraph

A **narrative paragraph** describes an event, feeling, or experience of the writer. It is often written in story form with details about events.

Look at the excerpt from "Confessions of an ESL Teacher." Who is speaking in this writing? How does the writer refer to herself? What is the topic?

> I confess. I am a logophile. That means I am a word lover. The words above are from my word collection. I am a compulsive word collector. With all my hundreds of words, I must be a terrific ESL teacher.

Now look at the first few sentences of this piece of student writing. Who is speaking in this writing? What does he or she call himself or herself? What experience is the writer describing?

> My family didn't take me to school until I was ten years old. When I went to my class, all the students could already read. Some students laughed at me because I didn't read or talk at school and I was old. I didn't want to go back to school because I felt very bad.

In narrative paragraphs, writers usually refer to themselves as *I*. The journal questions in this chapter ask *you* about your language learning. This means you will write a narrative paragraph telling about a feeling of yours about language learning or an event or experience in your life related to language learning.

Getting Started

Getting started is often the hardest part of a writing assignment for many students. In this chapter, your goal is to learn about selecting your topic.

There are many different kinds of pre-writing activities to help you get started. Brainstorming, freewriting, and keeping a journal are a few of the pre-writing strategies writers use. They are all about collecting and selecting ideas. For your writing assignments in this book, you will use your writing journals as a starting point. Your writing journal responses are a collection of ideas from your own knowledge and experiences, your reading, and your discussions.

Finding Your Topic

Return to your writing journal, and reread your responses to the opening journal questions for Readings 1, 2, and 3. Choose one of the journal questions and your response to it as your starting point. Choose the question and response with which you will be most comfortable. Here are some questions that will help you choose:

- For which question did I write the most?
- Which question was the most interesting to me?
- Which question was the easiest for me to write about?
- Which question did I like and enjoy the most?

Think about the outlines you completed after each reading selection. Identify the topic and main idea of the paragraph you are going to write.

The topic: _____

Write a word or phrase.

The main idea: _____

Write a sentence.

_____

Write your topic and main idea at the top of a piece of paper. Reread your journal response for the question you chose. Consider which ideas to use and which to eliminate. You can circle or highlight the ideas that you want to include. After your main idea sentence, list several ideas you want to include in your paragraph. These ideas are the support for your main idea.

Ideas to include:

a.

b.

c.

d.

e.

Work with a classmate, and describe what you want to say in your writing. Together, look at the ideas you have selected from your journal. Are there ideas that you should eliminate? Are there some ideas to add? Switch roles and help your partner.

Time to Write

When you are satisfied with your topic and the list of ideas, write a first draft without worrying about mechanics or correctness. Simply try to get your ideas on paper. Return to your journal and your list of ideas anytime you need to. Exchange paragraphs with a classmate. Read your classmate's paragraph and respond to it. Think about what the paragraph says rather than the mechanics. Does the paragraph give the meaning your classmate intended? Help each other by checking for meaning and making suggestions. Consider your classmate's response, and make any changes that you think will improve the reader's understanding. Make a final copy to turn in to your instructor.

2

How Clean Should We Be?

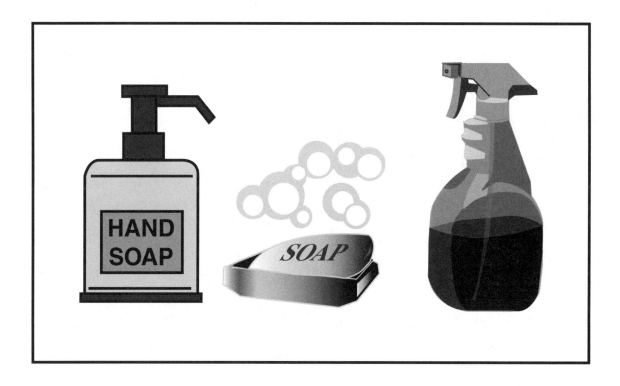

"Children should be clean enough to be healthy and dirty enough to be happy."

—American folk wisdom

Think about the Topic

- Why is it important to keep your hands clean?
- How does cleanliness affect a person's health?
- What does the quote mean to you?

Reading 1: Antibacterial Soap a Waste of Time

In Your Writing Journal

Write this question at the top of a new page in your writing journal. Then write an answer based on your own knowledge and experience. Write as much as you can. Save your writing journal so you can add to it later.

What kinds of things should people do to be sure they are clean and healthy?

Before You Read...

Discuss with Your Classmates

- What are the advantages of frequent hand-washing and good personal hygiene?
- What kinds of products do you use for hand-washing and personal hygiene?
- How often and when should you wash your hands?
- How do you decide which soap to buy for hand-washing and bathing?
- Which is better: antibacterial hand and body soaps or plain soaps? Why?

Consider This Background Information

- Bacteria are microorganisms (invisible living things) that are everywhere.
- Bacteria can cause illnesses, such as ear infections, strep throat, and food poisoning.
- Not all bacteria cause illnesses. Some are necessary for good health.
- Antibacterial products, sometimes called antimicrobial products, kill and control bacteria.
- Triclosan is an antibiotic. It is the most common ingredient used in antibacterial products to kill bacteria.
- In the mid-1990s there were a few dozen antibacterial products. Now there are more than 700 antibacterial products, including soaps, laundry detergents, baby toys, toothbrushes, and cutting boards.
- Barbara Ingham is a professor and food science extension specialist at the University of Wisconsin in Madison.
- Her newsletters provide current information about many different health issues.
- One of her duties is to provide the community with consumer education programs.

Visit Your Writing Journal

What new ideas from your discussion can you add to your writing journal?

Step 1: Read for the Main Idea

First, read the selection quickly. Read it from beginning to end, and try to understand the writer's main idea and a few supporting ideas. Notice that some AWL words for vocabulary study are underlined. Underline any other words that are unfamiliar to you. Don't stop reading to look them up. Complete the outline at the end of the selection.

Antibacterial Soap a Waste of Time

Barbara Ingham, Food Science Extension Specialist,
University of Wisconsin (Madison)

marginalia

We've known for some time that antibacterial soaps may be harmful for the environment. Now new research says that antibacterial soaps may not provide any extra health protection. At a meeting of the Infectious Diseases Society of America, researchers learned that antibacterial products are generally a waste of time. They also learned that it is difficult to buy soap in the United States that is not antibacterial. Researchers from the Columbia University School of Nursing in New York evaluated antibacterial soap and regular soap. The primary caretakers in 222 New York City households were involved in the study. Half of the households received antibacterial soap for daily hand-washing, and half were given plain soap. Neither soap was labeled. The researchers tested the two groups for bacteria after one year. The researchers found that antibacterial soap isn't any more effective than plain soap for hand-washing. The group that used the antibacterial soap did not have fewer bacteria on their hands. Soap and water works by simply washing away germs. For daily hygiene, washing your hands with regular soap is fine.

The researchers say it is important to wash hands properly. This means washing and scrubbing all surfaces: fingers, the backs of hands, between fingers, wrists, and under fingernails and jewelry.

A survey has shown that 75 percent of liquid hand soaps and 30 percent of bar soaps contain antibacterial ingredients. This sounds like good news, but it's not. Scientists and health-care professionals are concerned about the increase of anti-bacterial ingredients in personal and home cleaning products. Heavy use of antibacterial products may lead to the growth of antibiotic-resistant bacteria. These resistant bacteria are sometimes called "super-germs" because they are hard to kill. Most antibacterial soaps contain an antibacterial ingredient called triclosan. Triclosan is actually an antibiotic (medicine). Dr. Stuart Levy, a professor and researcher at Tufts University Medical School, has studied triclosan. He reported that when triclosan kills normal (nonresistant) bacteria, it is easier for "super germs" to survive. When this happens, it becomes more difficult to treat and cure infections in humans.

Overall, some evidence shows that antibacterial soaps may be useful in health-care situations if extra protection against bacteria is needed. However, recent studies have shown that for most consumers antibacterial products are no more effective than plain soap. Their use may even lead to serious medical problems for doctors.

Source: Adapted from *Food Science Newsletter,* University of Wisconsin, January 2003.

Based on your first reading, complete this outline:

The topic: _____

                              Write a word or phrase.

The main idea: *Antibacterial products may not* _____

                              Complete the sentence starter about the main idea.

                              _____

Some supporting ideas: _____

                              Write a different phrase or sentence on each line.

                              _____

                              _____

Do the supporting ideas help prove the main idea?

Step 2: Read for New Words

Return to Appendix A to review vocabulary-building strategies.

AWL Words to Know

These AWL words in order of appearance are underlined in the reading selection. Add them to your vocabulary journal.

environment	survey	overall
research	normal	evidence
primary	survive	consumers

Next, add any unfamiliar words that you underlined in Reading 1.

Follow these steps to complete your vocabulary journal:

1. Write the word and the sentence in the reading containing the word.
2. Note what part of speech the word should be based on its place in the sentence.
3. Guess the meaning of the word based on the sentence's meaning and the main idea of the reading selection.

4. Discuss your guess with your instructor and classmates, and confirm your guess by looking up the word in the dictionary. Add any notes that will help you remember the meaning of the word.

5. Use the word in your own original sentence.

6. Gloss the reading selection before reading it a second time.

Step 3: Read for Answers

Reread Reading 1, and add marginalia in the wide right-hand margin. Then return to the reading to find the information that you need to complete this exercise. Prepare to discuss your answers.

1. What two things did researchers learn at the meeting of the Infectious Diseases Society of America?

2. What did researchers from the Columbia University School of Nursing find out about antibacterial and plain soap?

3. What is *triclosan?* (See Consider This Background Information on page 32.)

4. What are *super-germs?*

5. What happens if it becomes easy for *super-germs* to survive?

Step 4: Read between the Lines

Do you think the writer of Reading 1 would agree or disagree with these statements? Return to the reading to discover the writer's opinion, and then circle A for agree or D for disagree. Prepare to give reasons for your answers. Remember to think about the <u>writer's opinion</u>, not your own opinion.

1. Hand-washing is the best way to avoid germs.   A   D

2. Antibacterial soaps help people stay healthy.   A   D

3. Health-care professionals should use antibacterial soaps.   A   D

4. Consumers should use antibacterial soaps.   A   D

5. People should always keep antibacterial soap in the kitchen and in the bathroom.   A   D

Step 5: Respond to the Reading

Reflect on your own knowledge and experience, and answer the questions. Remember to think about <u>your own opinions</u>. Be ready to discuss your answers.

1. Why do consumers buy more antibacterial soap than plain soap?

2. Will you buy antibacterial soap to use in your home? Why or why not?

3. What would you teach a young child about washing his or her hands?

Return to Your Writing Journal

Return to your writing journal, and review your response to the opening question for Reading 1. What new ideas and opinions do you have now? What new information have you learned about antibacterial soaps? Has this new information changed your opinion about using antibacterial products? Add your new thoughts to your response. Write as much as you can.

Reading 2: What the SDA Says about Antibacterial Products

In Your Writing Journal

Write this question at the top of a new page in your writing journal. Then write an answer based on your own knowledge and experience. Write as much as you can. Save your writing journal so you can add to it later.

> Are antibacterial cleaning products better than plain cleaning products? Why or why not?

Before You Read...

Discuss with Your Classmates

- How do people become ill?
- What is the best way to avoid germs? What do you do to avoid a cold?
- How did people prevent illnesses and diseases in the past?
- What are the advantages of a clean home?
- What kinds of cleaning products do you use to clean your home?
- What are the best products for home cleaning?

Consider This Background Information

- The Soap and Detergent Association (SDA) is a non-profit association. More than 100 North American manufacturers of cleaning products belong to the SDA.
- The SDA is involved in research, government affairs, consumer education, and public relations.
- The SDA provides information for consumers on its website, *www.cleaning101.com*.
- Some of the topics on the SDA website are proper hand-washing, safe food-handling practices, and facts and research about antibacterial products.

- Here are a few facts about germs from the SDA website:
  - There are more bacteria than any other type of organism; there can be as many as 2.5 million bacteria in one gram of soil.
  - Germs are most often spread by hands through person-to-person contact.
  - Germs can enter our bodies through the mouth, nose, eyes, and breaks in the skin without our even knowing we've been infected.
  - Americans spend about $5 billion each year on their colds, about $3 billion on doctors' visits, and $2 billion on treatments.
  - An estimated 60 million days of school and 50 million days of work are lost annually because of the common cold.
  - Some germs can live on dry surfaces (such as toys) for several hours and moist surfaces (like bathroom sinks) for up to three days.
  - The average kitchen dishcloth can contain 4 billion living germs.

Visit Your Writing Journal

What new ideas from your discussion can you add to your writing journal?

Step 1: Read for the Main Idea

First, read the selection quickly. Read it from beginning to end, and try to understand the writer's main idea and a few supporting ideas. Notice that some AWL words for vocabulary study are underlined. Underline any other words that are unfamiliar to you. Don't stop reading to look them up. Complete the outline at the end of the selection.

The reading selections that follow are from the SDA website. They are part of the SDA's consumer information program.

Antibacterial Products Provide Extra Protection against Germs

marginalia

Personal hygiene and regular housecleaning are essential to good health. Frequent hand-washing is key to preventing the spread of microorganisms (also known as microbes or germs) that cause many common illnesses. And regular cleaning of surfaces in the home removes dirt and food particles on which germs can grow.

Personal cleansing and household cleaning products that contain an active antibacterial or antimicrobial ingredient provide extra protection against germs, including those that may cause disease. That's because their active ingredient helps them go beyond simple cleaning to kill or control the growth of microorganisms. (The words *antibacterial* and *antimicrobial* are often used interchangeably. Strictly speaking, however, *antimicrobial* means activity against a wide variety of microorganisms, while *antibacterial* refers to activity against bacteria.) Together with good cleaning habits and practices, these products play an important <u>role</u> in helping to prevent germs from spreading.

Source: from *www.cleaning101.com.*

The next section is written as a question-and-answer chart. Organizations often share information this way because many people have asked the same questions.

FAQs about Antibacterial Soaps

Q	What is the main difference between plain soaps and antibacterial soaps used in the home?
A	The main difference is that antibacterial soaps contain a special ingredient for controlling germs. When washing with an antibacterial soap, a very small amount of antibacterial ingredient is deposited on the skin that keeps the number of germs at a <u>significantly</u> reduced level for an extended <u>period</u> of time. Washing with plain soap <u>initially</u> removes some germs, but the germs left on the hands can quickly regrow and increase in number.
Q	What germs do antibacterial soaps kill?
A	Antibacterial soaps kill or <u>inhibit</u> bacteria that cause odor, skin infections, food poisoning, intestinal illnesses and other commonly <u>transmitted</u> diseases. Their effectiveness depends on the antibacterial ingredient, its <u>concentration</u>, its <u>contact</u> time on the skin and the product <u>formulation</u>.
Q	Who should use antibacterial soaps?
A	Antibacterial soaps provide extra protection against bacteria that may cause many common illnesses. Consumers looking for additional protection before preparing and eating meals, after using the bathroom, diapering a child, after playing with a pet or when caring for the sick may want to use an antibacterial soap.

Q	Are deodorant soaps the same as antibacterial soaps?
A	No. A deodorant soap is a cosmetic product intended for washing the body to <u>eliminate</u> odors. A deodorant soap may or may not contain an ingredient that kills or inhibits the growth of odor-causing bacteria.
Q	Why are so many antibacterial soaps on the market now?
A	Soaps intended to kill or inhibit the growth of odor-causing bacteria have been marketed since the 1920s. Greater consumer concern over health risks from germs has <u>generated</u> increased demand for new antibacterial hand and body wash products.

Source: from *www.cleaning101.com.*

Based on your first reading, complete this outline:

The topic: _____

Write a word or phrase.

The main idea: *The SDA believes that* _____

Complete the sentence about the main idea.

_____

Some supporting ideas: _____

Write a different phrase or sentence on each line.

_____

_____

Do the supporting ideas help prove the main idea?

Step 2: Read for New Words

Return to Appendix A to review vocabulary-building strategies.

AWL Words to Know

These AWL words in order of appearance are underlined in the reading selection. Add them to your vocabulary journal.

role	initially	concentration	eliminate
significantly	inhibit	contact	generated
period	transmitted	formulation	

Next add any unfamiliar words that you underlined in Reading 2.

Follow these steps to complete your vocabulary journal:

1. Write the word and the sentence in the reading containing the word.

2. Note what part of speech the word should be based on its place in the sentence.

3. Guess the meaning of the word based on the sentence's meaning and the main idea of the reading selection.

4. Discuss your guess with your instructor and classmates, and confirm your guess by looking up the word up in the dictionary. Add any notes that will help you remember the meaning of the word.

5. Use the word in your own original sentence.

6. Gloss the reading selection before reading it a second time.

Step 3: Read for Answers

Reread Reading 2, and add marginalia in the wide right-hand margin. Then return to the reading to find the information that you need to complete this exercise. Prepare to discuss your answers.

Is the statement true (T), false (F), or impossible (I) to know for sure from the reading selection?

_____ 1. Antibacterial soaps contain special ingredients that are not in plain soaps.

_____ 2. Personal cleaning and household cleansing products contain the same anti-bacterial ingredient.

_____ 3. Deodorant soaps do not always contain antibacterial ingredients.

_____ 4. Consumers buy more antibacterial soap than plain or deodorant soap.

_____ 5. The number of germs on a person's hands can increase after washing with plain soap.

Step 4: Read between the Lines

Do you think the SDA would agree or disagree with these statements? Return to the reading to discover the writer's opinion, and then circle A for agree or D for disagree. Prepare to give reasons for your answers. Remember to think about the writer's opinion, not your own opinion.

1. Hand-washing with any kind of soap is the best way to avoid germs.   A   D

2. Antibacterial soaps help people stay healthy.   A   D

3. Health-care professionals should use antibacterial soaps.   A   D

4. Consumers should use antibacterial soaps.   A   D

5. People should always keep antibacterial soap in the kitchen and   A   D
   in the bathroom.

Step 5: Respond to the Reading

Reflect on your own knowledge and experience, and answer the questions. Remember to think about your own opinions. Be ready to discuss your answers.

1. Think about who belongs to the SDA (see Consider This Background Information on pages 38 and 39). Why would the SDA support the use of antibacterial soaps and other cleaning products?

2. Barbara Ingram and the SDA report different findings about the effectiveness of antibacterial products. Which source do you trust more? Why?

Return to Your Writing Journal

Return to your writing journal, and review your response to the opening question for Reading 2. What new ideas and opinions do you have now? Have you changed your opinion about using antibacterial products? Add your new thoughts to your response. Write as much as you can.

Writing Workshop:
The Academic Essay and Paragraph

Writing is the backbone of communication in the academic setting, especially between instructor and student. Instructors will ask you to write essays to show what you have learned and understood. Your essays will be made up of related paragraphs about a particular subject. Because paragraphs are the most important building blocks of an essay, it is important to be able to write good paragraphs before moving on to essays. Once you can write clear, well-developed paragraphs, it will be easy to move on to writing essays in your more advanced ESL classes and other college classes.

Academic Paragraph Structure

A paragraph is a **group of sentences** that are related to each other. In academic English, each paragraph develops just **one main idea.** The main idea is stated in the **topic sentence,** which is often the first sentence of the paragraph. This sentence tells the reader what the paragraph is about and what the writer's idea or attitude about the topic is. The writer's idea or attitude is called the **controlling idea** because it controls what the writer will include in the paragraph. The sentences that follow the topic sentence are called **supporting sentences** because they support (prove or explain) the main idea of the paragraph with specific facts, examples, descriptions, or a story. This group of sentences is sometimes called the **body** of the paragraph. It is important that all the support sentences are more specific than the topic sentence and that all of them directly support the main idea. The only sentence that may be as general as or more general than the topic sentence is the **concluding sentence,** the last sentence of the paragraph. The concluding sentence may summarize the main idea for the reader and remind the reader of the writer's attitude once more. When a paragraph includes a clear topic sentence, support sentences, and a concluding sentence, it is easy for a reader to follow and understand.

From Writer to Reader

As a writer, it is your job to help the reader understand what you are saying.

The reader needs:	The writer uses:
• to know the topic	• a topic sentence
• to know the writer's attitude about the topic	• a controlling idea in the topic sentence
• to understand the writer's attitude through information	• several support sentences
• to know that the paragraph is complete	• a concluding sentence

Remember that your purpose as a writer is to help the reader understand exactly what you are saying in your paragraph.

Appearance and Format

Paragraphs can be easily identified by their appearance. Handwritten paragraphs should be written on lined 8½" × 11" notebook paper. There should be a thin, faint vertical line on the left side of the paper. This line marks the left margin. Each line of writing, except the first line, begins next to this line. The first sentence begins after a blank space called an indentation. The indentation is approximately the width of your thumb, five letter spaces. The indentation tells the reader that a new paragraph has begun. All other lines (not sentences) of writing begin next to the left margin line. The right margin should be approximately the same size as the right, but it will be slightly uneven. Each new sentence begins after the ending punctuation mark of the sentence before it. New sentences do not begin on a new line.

Word-processed paragraphs may be indented in the same way as handwritten paragraphs. Sometimes an extra blank line separates one word-processed paragraph from another. This space alerts the reader that a new paragraph is about to begin. The side margins are set for 1" or 1.25". The top and bottom margins are usually set for 1". College instructors often give students specific directions about margins, spacing, font, and font size. See these three variations:

①

Indented handwritten topic sentence. Handwritten support sentence. Handwritten support sentence. Handwritten support sentence. Handwritten support sentence. Handwritten support sentence. Handwritten support sentence. Handwritten support sentence. Handwritten concluding sentence.

New paragraph topic sentence.

②

Indented word-processed topic sentence. Word-processed support sentence. Word-processed support sentence. Word-processed support sentence. Word-processed support sentence. Word-processed support sentence. Word-processed support sentence. Word-processed support sentence. Word-processed concluding sentence.

New paragraph topic sentence.

③

Non-indented word-processed topic sentence. Word-processed support sentence. Word-processed support sentence. Word-processed support sentence. Word-processed support sentence. Word-processed support sentence. Word-processed support sentence. Word-processed support sentence. Word-processed concluding sentence.

New paragraph topic sentence.

Writing Activity 1: An Example of an Academic Paragraph

① Children need to be exposed to bacteria when they are young. ② At birth, a baby's immune system is not ready to fight bacteria, so the immune system has to learn to recognize and fight bacteria. ③ This learning occurs every time a baby is exposed to bacteria or germs. ④ Young children who have older siblings or attend daycare are exposed to more infections and germs than children who are not around other children. ⑤ Children who live on farms or have pets are also exposed to more germs. ⑥ Consequently, these children have fewer allergies, skin problems, and cases of asthma when they are older. ⑦ Furthermore, researchers found that children who had daily baths and washed their hands more than five times a day had 25 percent more cases of allergies and asthma. ⑧ Overall, exposure to bacteria at a young age makes children healthier later in life.

For each item, write the circled number of the sentences that fit into each catagory:

Topic sentence: _____

Body sentences: _____

Concluding sentence: _____

The Topic Sentence: A Closer Look

A well-written paragraph has a clearly stated **topic sentence.** The topic sentence is an announcement of the topic of the paragraph and the writer's attitude about that topic.

The topic sentence:

- states the topic and the controlling idea
- focuses the paragraph and invites further exploration
- is a complete sentence

A simple formula for the topic sentence is:

a limited topic + a controlling idea = a topic sentence

Examine Topic Sentences

Look at this topic sentence from Reading 1:

> *Now new research says that antibacterial soaps may not provide any extra health protection.*

The topic is "research about antibacterial soaps." The controlling idea is "may not provide any extra health protection." All of the other sentences of the paragraph add support for the idea that the research says antibacterial products may not provide extra protection. The writer does not write about different kinds of antibacterial products, their ingredients, sales and advertising of antibacterial products, or anything else not related to the controlling idea.

Writing Activity 2: Practice Identifying Topics and Controlling Ideas

1. Circle the topic of each of these topic sentences. Underline the idea that tells the writer's attitude. This is the controlling idea and will help the reader know what to expect.
   a. Americans are too concerned about cleanliness.

   b. Frequent hand-washing is the best way to prevent the spread of germs that cause illnesses.

2. Add a controlling idea to each sentence starter to make a good topic sentence.
   a. After scientists discovered that bacteria caused illnesses....

   b. Manufacturers of antibacterial products....

Writing Activity 3: Practice Writing Topic Sentences

Write a topic sentence for each paragraph.

1. _____

_____

The early Greeks did not use soap when they bathed. Instead, they cleaned their bodies with blocks of clay, sand, pumice, and ashes. Then they rubbed oil on their bodies. Sometimes they added ashes to the oil. Next they scraped off the oil and dirt with a metal instrument called a strigil. The early Greeks did not bathe to be clean; they bathed to improve their appearance.

2. _____

_____

First, wet your hands, and apply liquid or use a clean bar of soap. Place the bar of soap on a rack, and allow it to dry. Next, rub your hands together vigorously and scrub all surfaces. Continue doing this for 10–15 seconds or about the length of a little tune. It is the soap, combined with the scrubbing action, that helps dislodge and remove germs. Rinse well, and dry your hands. This is one of many suggestions the Centers for Disease Control and Prevention offers.

Writing Activity 4: Think about the Support Sentences of the Paragraph

Each sentence following the topic sentence, except the last sentence, should give new information that supports the writer's attitude about the topic.

Look at the same topic sentences, and identify several ideas that would provide support. Facts, details, descriptions, and examples are some ways to give support.

1. Americans are too concerned about cleanliness.

2. Frequent hand-washing is the best way to prevent the spread of germs that cause illnesses.

Time to Write

Choose Your Topic

Return to your writing journal, and review your responses to the opening questions for Readings 1 and 2. Choose one response to develop in a paragraph.

Start Your Paragraph

Identify the topic of your paragraph. To write your topic sentence, add a controlling idea. A good way to do this is to write a one-sentence answer to the writing journal question.

Suppose you have decided to develop your response for Question 2, "Are antibacterial cleaning products better than plain cleaning products? Why or why not?"

Your one-sentence answer might be:

Antibacterial products are better than plain products because they provide more protection from germs.

Return to your writing journal to gather ideas that support your topic sentence. Make a list of ideas you want to include as support. Your list can be written as words or phrases. (You will learn about support in Chapter 3.) You can return to the reading selections and your writing journal for more ideas.

Write Your First Draft

When you are satisfied with your topic sentence and list of ideas, write a first draft without worrying about mechanics or correctness. Simply try to get your ideas on paper. Return to your writing journal and your list of ideas anytime you need to.

Share Your Paragraph with a Classmate

Make a photocopy of your paragraph to use for editing with a partner. Highlight the topic sentence. Exchange copies with a classmate.

Think about what readers need in order to understand your meaning. First, they need to know the topic and your attitude or feelings about it. Consider your classmate's topic sentence before reading the entire paragraph. Use these questions to evaluate the topic sentence:

- Does it identify the topic?
- Does it identify the writer's attitude about the topic?
- After reading the topic sentence, does the reader have a general idea about what to expect in the paragraph?

Now, read the entire paragraph and respond to it. Think about what the paragraph says rather than the mechanics. Does the paragraph give the meaning your classmate intended? Help each other by checking for meaning and making suggestions. Consider your classmate's responses, and make any changes that you think will improve the reader's understanding. When you are satisfied with your paragraph, make a final copy to turn in to your instructor.

3

To Tell the Truth and Nothing But

Ma'at, Egyptian Goddess of Truth

Courtesy of Jan Fleck

> "If it is not right, do not do it;
> if it is not true, do not say it."
>
> —Marcus Aurelius,
> Roman emperor, 161–180 CE

Think about the Topic

- How do you define honesty?
- What does the quote by Marcus Aurelius mean to you?
- In your opinion, is anything more important than honesty? In other words, is there anything that would cause you to behave dishonestly?

Reading 1: Ouch! Students Getting Stung Trying to Find $$$ for College

In Your Writing Journal

Write this question at the top of a new page in your writing journal. Then, write an answer based on your own knowledge and experience. Write as much as you can. Save your writing journal so you can add to it later.

What is the purpose of advertising? How does it affect consumers?

Before You Read...

Discuss with Your Classmates

- What are some things businesses do to get people to buy their products or services?
- Have you ever been misled by advertisements and promises made by a business?
- How can you protect yourself against dishonest and unfair businesses and advertisers?
- What kinds of advertisements might be directed at college students?

Consider This Background Information

- The Federal Trade Commission (FTC) is a government organization that enforces federal consumer protection laws.
- It has two goals:
  - to protect consumers from frauds and unfair business practices
  - to provide information to help consumers identify, stop, and avoid frauds and unfair business practices
- The FTC states that "unfair or deceptive acts or practices are unlawful." It also prohibits false or misleading advertisements.
- The FTC keeps an online list of complaints. This list is used by law enforcement agencies.
- Each year the FTC ships more than six million copies of its consumer and business education materials.

- The FTC offers several hundred publications for consumers. Some examples include "Avoiding Credit and Charge Card Fraud," "International Telephone Number Scams," and "Buying a Used Car."
- "Ouch! Students Getting Stung Trying to Find $$$ for College" is an FTC publication warning college students about deceptive scholarship offers.

Visit Your Writing Journal
What new ideas from your discussion can you add to your writing journal?

Step 1: Read for the Main Idea

First, read the selection quickly. Read it from beginning to end, and try to understand the writer's main idea and a few supporting ideas. Notice that some AWL words for vocabulary study are underlined. You should also underline any other words that are unfamiliar to you. Don't stop reading to look them up. Complete the outline at the end of the selection.

Ouch! Students Getting Stung Trying to Find $$$ for College

marginalia

Need money for college? Doesn't everybody? With tuition bills skyrocketing, and room and board going through the roof, students and their families are looking for creative ways to finance a college education. Unfortunately, in their efforts to pay the bills, many of them are falling prey to scholarship and financial aid scams.

According to the Federal Trade Commission, unscrupulous companies guarantee or promise scholarships, grants, or fantastic financial aid packages. Many use high-pressure sales pitches at seminars where you're required to pay immediately or risk losing out on the "opportunity."

Some unscrupulous companies guarantee that they can get scholarships on behalf of students or award them "scholarships" in exchange for an advance fee. Most offer a "money back guarantee" but attach conditions that make it impossible to get the refund. Others provide nothing for the student's advance fee—not even a list of <u>potential</u> sources; still others tell students they've been selected as "finalists" for awards that require an up-front fee. Sometimes, these companies ask for a student's checking account to "confirm eligibility," then debit the account without the student's <u>consent</u>. Other companies quote only a relatively small "monthly" or "weekly" fee and then ask for authorization to debit your checking account for an undetermined length of time.

The FTC cautions students to look and listen for these tell-tale lines:

- "The scholarship is guaranteed or your money back."
- "You can't get this information anywhere else."
- "I just need your credit card or bank account number to hold this scholarship."
- "We'll do all the work."
- "The scholarship will cost some money."
- "You've been selected" by a "national foundation" to receive a scholarship or "You're a finalist" in a contest you never entered.

If you attend a seminar on financial aid or scholarships, follow these steps:

- Take your time. Don't be rushed into paying at the seminar. Avoid high-pressure sales pitches that require you to buy now or risk losing out on the opportunity. Solid opportunities are not sold through nerve-racking tactics.
- <u>Investigate</u> the organization you're considering paying for help. Talk to a guidance counselor or financial aid advisor before spending your money. You may be able to get the same help for free.
- Be wary of "success stories" or testimonials of extraordinary success—the seminar operation may have paid shills to give glowing stories. Instead, ask for a list of at least three local families who've used the services in the last year. Ask each if they're satisfied with the products and services received.

■ Be cautious about purchasing from seminar representatives who are <u>reluctant</u> to answer questions or who give evasive answers to your questions. Legitimate business people are more than willing to give you information about their service.

■ Ask how much money is charged for the service, what services will be performed, and what the company's refund <u>policy</u> is. Get this information in writing. Keep in mind that you may never recoup the money you give to an unscrupulous operator, <u>despite</u> stated refund policies.

The FTC says many legitimate companies advertise that they can get students <u>access</u> to lists of scholarships in exchange for an advance fee. Other legitimate services charge an advance fee to compare a student's profile with a database of scholarship opportunities and provide a list of awards for which a student may qualify. And there are scholarship search engines on the Internet. The difference: Legitimate companies *never* guarantee or promise scholarships or grants.

Based on your first reading, complete this outline:

The topic: _____
Write a word or phrase.

The main idea: _____
Write a complete sentence that tells the main idea.

_____

Some supporting ideas: _____
Write a different phrase or sentence on each line.

_____

_____

Do the supporting ideas help prove the main idea?

Step 2: Read for New Words

Return to Appendix A to review vocabulary-building strategies.

AWL Words to Know

These AWL words and phrases in order of appearance are underlined in the reading selection. Add them to your vocabulary journal.

creative	(on) behalf	consent	despite
aid	fee	investigate	access
guarantee	attach	reluctant	
grants	potential	policy	

Next, add any unfamiliar words that you underlined in Reading 1.

Follow these steps to complete your vocabulary journal:

1. Write the word and the sentence in the reading containing the word.

2. Note what part of speech the word should be based on its place in the sentence.

3. Guess the meaning of the word based on the sentence's meaning and the main idea of the reading selection.

4. Discuss your guess with your instructor and classmates, and confirm your guess by looking up the word in the dictionary. Add any notes that will help you remember the meaning of the word.

5. Use the word in your own original sentence.

6. Gloss the reading selection before reading it a second time.

Step 3: Read for Answers

Reread Reading 1, and add marginalia in the wide right-hand margin. Then return to the reading to find the information that you need to complete this exercise. Prepare to discuss your answers.

1. What are some of the ways unscrupulous companies get money from students seeking scholarships?

2. What are some things legitimate companies can do for students for a fee?

3. What is the major difference between a legitimate and an unscrupulous company offering scholarship assistance?

Step 4: Read between the Lines

For these questions, pretend that you are the writer of the FTC material you have just read. Remember to think like a writer of FTC materials. Prepare to give reasons for your answers.

1. This information is available in printed form and on the Internet. Why should it be on the Internet as well as in printed form?

2. This quote is from a printed FTC publication. What is the purpose of including stories of people's experiences?

> An Oregon family paid $179 for a "guaranteed" scholarship of at least $1,000 to help pay for their son's college tuition bill. Instead, they received a list of 27 scholarship programs for which they could apply, some with deadlines long past. The same list was available in his high school library for free.

Step 5: Respond to the Reading

Reflect on your own knowledge and experience, and answer the questions. Remember to think about <u>your own opinions</u>. Be ready to discuss your answers.

1. What information in this reading selection is most useful to you? Most surprising?

2. You can probably think of many questions you would ask a scholarship company representative. Write the three questions that you consider the most important to protect yourself from scholarship and financial aid scams.

   a.

   b.

   c.

Return to Your Writing Journal

Return to your writing journal, and review your response to the opening question for Reading 1. What new ideas do you have about advertising now? Add your new thoughts to your response. Write as much as you can.

Reading 2: Academic Integrity

In Your Writing Journal

Write this question at the top of a new page in your writing journal. Then write an answer based on your own knowledge and experience. Write as much as you can. Save your writing journal so you can add to it later.

> Today there is more cheating in American high schools and colleges than at any other time in the past. Why and how can the amount of cheating be reduced?

Before You Read...

Discuss with Your Classmates

- What does *integrity* mean? What does *academic integrity* mean?
- How would you define cheating? What kinds of behavior are considered cheating?
- How common is cheating in schools in your native country?
- Why do students cheat?

Consider This Background Information

- Plagiarizing is copying another person's words, ideas, or work and acting like they are your own.
- Plagiarizing is a serious form of dishonesty in the United States. Several American journalists and authors have lost their jobs as a result of plagiarizing.
- The Center for Academic Integrity (CAI) was founded by Donald McCabe at Duke University in 1992. It promotes anti-cheating campaigns on more than 200 college campuses. The CAI is supported by the John Templeton Foundation and the William and Flora Hewlett Foundation. It published *The Fundamental Values of Academic Integrity: Honesty, Trust, Respect, Fairness, Responsibility*.
- The Josephson Institute of Ethics, founded by Michael Josephson in 1987, offers integrity training programs to businesses, government agencies, nonprofit organizations, and schools to promote honesty. Every two years, the Josephson Institue of Ethics releases the *Report Card on the Ethics of American Youth*. It has also developed a special program called Character Counts! and published *Changing Cheaters: Promoting Integrity and Preventing Academic Dishonesty*.

Visit Your Writing Journal

What new ideas from your discussion can you add to your writing journal?

Step 1: Read for the Main Idea

First, read the selection quickly. Read it from beginning to end, and try to understand the writer's main idea and a few supporting ideas. Notice that some AWL words for vocabulary study are underlined. Underline any other words that are unfamiliar to you. Don't stop reading to look them up. Complete the outline at the end of the selection.

Academic Integrity

marginalia

(1) As long as there have been schools, tests, and homework, there has been academic dishonesty. Some students have always found ways to cheat. Now, educators say cheating is at an all-time high in high schools and colleges. They also identify new methods of cheating and new <u>attitudes</u> about cheating in today's students. Educators and organizations that <u>promote</u> <u>integrity</u> and study academic dishonesty are searching for explanations and solutions. They want to know how and why students cheat and what can be done about academic dishonesty.

(2) One organization, the Josephson Institute of <u>Ethics</u>, <u>conducted</u> a survey of more than 12,000 high school students in 2002. It found that 74 percent of students cheated on tests at least once during the school year, and 48 percent cheated twice or more. Stephen Davis, a professor at Emporia State University, has studied student attitudes for more than 15 years. He found research that <u>indicates</u> 18–23 percent of students cheated in 1941. Kevin Ryan, an ex-professor at Boston University, says he never saw or heard of cheating when he taught in the mid-1950s. He states, "There was such a strong attitude against it, it was clearly shameful." Today, even honor students cheat. More than 80 percent of high-achievers admit

to cheating. Other studies verify the increase of cheating.
Does this mean that today's students are more dishonest than
earlier <u>generations</u>? Most researchers agree that cheating has
increased, but Donald McCabe of the Center for Academic
Integrity, says another <u>phenomenon</u> has occurred. Students are
more willing to admit that they cheat because "cheating is just
not such a big deal to kids today."

(3) Studies on academic dishonesty have also examined the
way today's students cheat. In the past, cheating meant looking at another student's test paper, using forbidden materials,
writing notes on hands, and copying another student's homework. Nowadays, cheating is high-tech. <u>Technology</u> allows
students to receive answers from friends across the classroom
or even outside by using electronic <u>devices</u> such as palm pilots,
cell phones, pagers, and tiny video cameras. Students program
calculators to display formulas and other unauthorized information but add another program to show an empty memory
if instructors check. Other high-tech cheating involves the use
of the Internet. The so-called "new plagiarism"—downloading
parts or entire essays from the Internet—is the most common
form of high-tech cheating. Many students even pay for essays
from illegitimate online sources; others simply "cut-and-paste"
information from the Internet.

(4) The reasons for student cheating are <u>varied</u>. Some educators say students are lazy or too busy. Cheating takes only
a few minutes; studying takes many hours. Some students
feel pressure from high-stakes tests for which they are often
unprepared. They know that poor test results may <u>eliminate</u>
opportunities such as attending college or moving to a higher
level. Some students fear failure. Others blame professors for
giving too much work, unfair tests, or grading unfairly. These
reasons explain individual student behavior, but there is a
more general and worrisome reason for cheating. This has
to do with a change in attitude. Many students don't believe

that cheating is really wrong. They see cheating as acceptable and necessary. Students caught cheating are not sorry for their behavior. One student said, "I would do it again."

(5) Researchers at the CAI and the Josephson Institute of Ethics think that there is a lack of integrity throughout American society. Michael Josephson blames adults for students' dishonest behavior. He says that adults cheat on taxes and campaign finances, coaches cheat in order to win. Children and students see adults placing more importance on success than honesty. They are simply copying the behavior and attitudes of adults. This makes it even harder to eliminate academic dishonesty.

(6) In his booklet, *Changing Cheaters: Promoting Integrity and Preventing Academic Dishonesty,* Josephson suggests many practical ways to prevent cheating, such as seating arrangements and watching students carefully. He also suggests the use of honor codes. An honor <u>code</u> is a set of rules for honest academic behavior. It includes <u>consequences</u> for breaking the rules. Many educators think that honor codes cannot change dishonest behavior, but McCabe has found that honor codes really do reduce academic dishonesty. His research shows less cheating in colleges with honor codes. He found that one in six students cheated several times at schools without honor codes, but only one in sixteen cheated several times at schools with honor codes. McCabe believes that it is not the honor code itself that reduces cheating. Instead, it is the communication about academic integrity and student involvement with honor codes that leads to a more honest student population. A more honest student population may be the best solution because these students are the parents of the future.

Based on your first reading, complete this outline:

The topic: _____

Write a word or phrase.

The main idea: _____

Write a complete sentence that tells the main idea.

_____

Some supporting ideas: _____

Write a different phrase or sentence on each line.

_____

_____

Do the supporting ideas help prove the main idea?

Step 2: Read for New Words

Return to Appendix A to review vocabulary-building strategies.

AWL Words to Know

These AWL words in order of appearance are underlined in the reading selection. Add them to your vocabulary journal.

attitude	ethics	generations	devices	code
promote	conducted	phenomenon	varied	consequence
integrity	indicates	technology	eliminate	

Next, add any unfamiliar words that you underlined in Reading 2.

Follow these steps to complete your vocabulary journal:

1. Write the word and the sentence in the reading containing the word.
2. Note what part of speech the word should be based on its place in the sentence.
3. Guess the meaning of the word based on the sentence's meaning and the main idea of the reading selection.

4. Discuss your guess with your instructor and classmates, and confirm your guess by looking up the word in the dictionary. Add any notes that will help you remember the meaning of the word.

5. Use the word in your own original sentence.

6. Gloss the reading selection before reading it a second time.

Step 3: Read for Answers

Reread Reading 2, and add marginalia in the wide right-hand margin. Then return to the reading to find the information that you need to complete this exercise. Prepare to discuss your answers.

1. Today's students cheat more than students in the past. How does the author prove this? Give examples.

2. How did students cheat in the past?

3. How do students cheat now?

4. Why do students cheat? List several reasons.

5. What is an honor code?

Step 4: Read between the Lines

Do you think the writer of Reading 2 would agree or disagree with these statements? Return to the reading to discover the writer's opinion, then circle A for agree or D for disagree. Prepare to give reasons for your answers. Remember to think about the <u>writer's opinion</u>, not your own opinion.

1. Adults and society are partly responsible for student cheating.   A   D

2. Academic dishonesty is a serious problem.   A   D

3. Students who admit to cheating are telling the truth.   A   D

4. Technology has made it easier to cheat.   A   D

5. An honor code may be the best way to reduce cheating because it changes both attitudes and behavior.   A   D

Step 5: Respond to the Reading

Reflect on your own knowledge and experience, and answer the questions. Remember to think about <u>your own opinions</u>. Be ready to discuss your answers.

 1. Consider this case, and answer the questions. Explain your answers.

> A few years ago, Christine Pelton, a high school science teacher in Piper, Kansas, figured out that 28 of the 118 students in her sophomore botany class had handed in plagiarized work on a major project. She failed them. Pelton claimed the students copied information directly from the Internet without properly citing the sources or rewriting the information in their own words. Some of their parents thought an F was too severe a punishment and complained to the school board. The parents claimed that the students didn't realize copying work off the Internet was plagiarism. (Plagiarize means to copy someone else's writing as if it were your own.) When the school board directed Pelton to change the grades, she resigned from her teaching job.

 a. Do you think the students knew they were plagiarizing when they copied from the Internet?

 b. Do you approve or disapprove of the parents' actions? Why?

 c. Do you approve or disapprove of the school board's actions? Why?

 d. Do you approve or disapprove of Pelton's decision to resign? Why?

 2. Readings 1 and 2 discuss dishonesty involving students. In each case of dishonesty, who is cheating? Who is being cheated?

Return to Your Writing Journal

Return to your writing journal, and review your response to the opening question for Reading 2. What new ideas do you have about cheating? What other reasons can you give for cheating? Can you think of additional ways to reduce cheating? Add your new thoughts to your response. Write as much as you can.

Writing Workshop: Paragraph Support Using Concrete and Specific Details

In Chapter 2, you studied academic paragraphs and learned about writing topic sentences. In this chapter you will learn to support your topic sentence with information that is **specific** and **concrete**.

Specific Support

Whereas a general statement describes a number of different things, people, places, or situations, specific support is a detail that describes a particular person, place, thing, or situation. Although a general word can be used accurately in many cases, a more **specific word** gives the reader a clearer picture of a particular case. For instance, *interesting* is a very general adjective to describe a movie. Many movies could be described as *interesting*. However, *humorous, frightening,* or *romantic* are more specific. A horror movie could be described as *frightening,* but a love story or comedy couldn't. *Picture* is a general noun. Many pieces of framed art could be called pictures. However, *photograph, painting,* or *drawing* are more specific. Only a picture created with a camera could be called a *photograph. Well* is a very general adverb. Many actions could be described as *well done.* However, *quickly, gracefully,* or *completely* are more specific. Only an action performed in less time than expected would be described as *quickly done.*

Writing Activity 1: Practice Being Specific

For each of these general words, write at least three more specific words. Use the same part of speech. For example, for a general verb write three more specific verbs, and for a general adjective write three more specific adjectives.

General Word	Specific Words
Examples: *relative* (noun) *go* (verb)	*aunt, uncle, cousin* *drive, walk, fly*
1. *building* (noun)	
2. *say* (verb)	
3. *school* (noun)	
4. *vehicle* (noun)	

Although a reader may agree with a general statement, like a paragraph's topic sentence, he or she is more likely to be convinced by a series of specific details that illustrate the statement. Consider this general statement: *Parking at Henderson Community College is a problem.* A student or employee of this college may agree or disagree based on his or her own experiences looking for a parking space on campus.

Now consider these specific details:

On average, there are more than 2,500 students attending classes between 8 AM and 12 PM weekdays. However, there are only 1,746 student parking spaces on campus. Parking permits cost students $15.00 per quarter, yet that permit does not guarantee that a morning student will have a parking space. In order to arrive on time to an 8 AM class, a student needs to get to campus earlier than 7:30 AM to look for one of the few remaining parking spaces. Students, who often are juggling work and family responsibilities along with their studies, may find it difficult to arrive 30 minutes early each day. Finally, searching for a parking space can be stressful and distracting when too few spaces are available. Students preparing for tests and working hard to meet assignment deadlines do not need additional stress or distraction caused by simply attempting to park their car.

An evening student, who may have little difficulty locating a parking space on campus, may initially disagree with the general statement, *Parking at Henderson Community College is a problem*, but may be persuaded by the specific details:

On average, there are more than 2,500 students attending classes between 8 AM and 12 PM weekdays. However, there are only 1,746 student parking spaces on campus.

A member of the Henderson College administration, who already knows that there are fewer parking spaces than there are morning students but also does not agree that a "problem" exists, may be persuaded by the specific details about the inconvenience and stress the lack of parking spaces causes students.

An academic writer needs to do more than simply make a statement. He or she must support that statement—that is, prove it, explain it, or illustrate it with plenty of specific details. It is as though the general statement, or topic sentence, is simply the destination of a trip, and the specific support is the map that shows how to get there. For the reader to agree with or even understand the writer's main idea, he or she must be permitted to consider the details, or take the trip and arrive at the destination. Academic writers who use plenty of specific support don't just **tell** their readers what they think. They **show** them. And in showing them, they are far more likely to **convince** them.

Take another look at Reading 2, "Academic Integrity." Note how the writer used specific detail to support more general statements. For instance, in paragraph 3 on page 62, the writer makes the general statement, "Nowadays, cheating is high-tech." A reader may not understand or believe this statement without the specific details that follow. The writer describes "high-tech" specifically as "allows students to receive answers from friends across the classroom or even outside by using electronic devices," and "calculators to display formulas and other unauthorized information." Even more specifically, the writer identifies "electronic devices" as "palm pilots, cell phones, pagers, and tiny video cameras."

Now look at paragraph 4 on pages 62–63. With what specific details does the writer support this general statement: "The reasons for student cheating are varied."

1. *lazy or too busy* _____

2. _____

3. _____

4. _____

5. _____

In paragraph 6 on page 63, what specific facts support the statement, "Many educators think that honor codes cannot change dishonest behavior, but McCabe has found that honor codes really do reduce academic dishonesty."

1. _____ *in schools without honor codes.*

2. _____ *in schools with honor codes.*

Review your responses to the Step 3 activities you completed after Readings 1 and 2, and note the use of specific details to support general statements.

Concrete Support

To be convincing, an academic writer must support topic sentences with plenty of specific detail. Detail can be either **abstract** or **concrete**. Abstract information consists of ideas that are understood without the use of the five physical senses. For instance, "knowledge" is real, yet it cannot be seen, heard, smelled, tasted, or touched. "Knowledge" is an abstract concept. "Courage" is another abstract concept. We may judge that someone has courage or demonstrates courage by his actions, yet we can't actually see his courage or weigh it on a scale. Because abstract ideas are understood differently by different readers, they must be illustrated with plenty of **concrete** information so that the reader can firmly grasp the writer's meaning. Concrete information is that which can be detected with the physical senses.

Consider this sentence:

He was nervous.

Nervous is an abstract adjective. Different readers will imagine the subject *he* differently. However, *nervous* can be illustrated with these concrete details:

He had sweaty palms, a racing heart, and two red cheeks.

Consider this sentence:

The stallion was beautiful.

Beautiful is another abstract adjective and is understood differently by different readers. However, when the concrete details are provided, it's easier to imagine:

The stallion had a glossy black coat, a long silky black tail, a smoothly combed mane, and a bright white blaze on his forehead.

Writing Activity 2: Practice

For each abstract word or phrase, write at least three concrete words or phrases that make the meaning clearer.

Abstract Phrase	Concrete Phrases
Examples:	
helpful teacher	*answers questions in class, stays after class to talk with students, helps students find solutions to problems*
learning a language	*talking with native speakers, listening to radio, watching TV, attending classes, reading and writing in the language, studying grammar rules*
1. valuable jewelry	
2. honesty	
3. technology	

In particular, readers of a different culture or first language need plenty of concrete information to ensure that they understand abstract ideas. Furthermore, concrete information and details that create a vivid sensory image in the reader's mind make the writer's points not only clear, but also more memorable.

Review Reading 1 in this chapter, "Ouch! Students Getting Stung Trying to Find $$$ for College." Note the writer's effective use of concrete detail to explain the abstract idea of unscrupulous. In paragraph three, the writer clarifies "unscrupulous companies" by using examples of behavior. What are some of the behaviors of an unscrupulous company?

1. *scholarship for advance fee* _____

2. *impossible to get refund* _____

3. _____

4. _____

5. _____

In paragraph 4, the writer provides further clarification with a list of statements that an unscrupulous company might make. From this list, a reader will clearly know when to question a company's legitimacy. Without these concrete details in paragraphs 3 and 4, the reader might complete the reading selection without understanding how to recognize an unscrupulous company. The message from the FTC would be missed.

Review your response to questions 1, 2, and 3 in Step 3. What concrete examples and details did you find that help you distinguish an unscrupulous company from a legitimate company?

After building an image of unscrupulous companies in the reader's mind, the writer clarifies another abstract adjective: legitimate. What concrete examples does the writer provide to clarify "legitimate" companies? Find them and list them here:

1. *access to lists of scholarships* _____

2. _____

3. _____

Writing Activity 3: Practice Revising for Concrete and Specific Details

With a partner, edit this sample paragraph. Underline all abstract words that need concrete explanation and put a star in each place where more specific detail could be added. Suggest some concrete and specific details to add.

> Advertisers often use deceptive advertisements to take advantage of consumers' feelings and desires. Advertisers know that American consumers want to look attractive, so they show attractive people wearing or using their products. These advertisements encourage consumers to believe they need a particular product to become attractive. Advertisers also know that consumers want to be thought of as successful. In addition to the desires for attractiveness and success, consumers want to be healthy. Smart consumers know that advertisers want them to think their products will make them attractive, successful, and healthy.

Remember: As a writer, you must help the reader understand exactly what you are saying in your paragraph. To do this, the main idea, stated in the topic sentence, must be developed. Thorough development is achieved by using specific and concrete details to support the topic sentence.

Time to Write

In this paragraph you will pay careful attention to the use of **specific** and **concrete** information to support your topic sentence. Keep in mind that the topic sentence tells the reader the main idea, and it is the most general sentence in a paragraph. All of the other sentences, except the concluding sentence, should provide concrete and specific information that explains the main idea.

Start Your Paragraph

Now return to your writing journal, and read over your responses to the opening journal questions for Readings 1 and 2. Choose one response to develop in a paragraph. Identify the topic of your paragraph and add a controlling idea. Write your topic sentence.

Return to your writing journal to gather details that support your topic sentence. Make a list of details to include as support. Examine each detail for specificity and concreteness.

Show your topic sentence to a classmate, but do not show your list of supporting details. Ask your partner:

What information should I include to convince you that my topic sentence is true?

What are some specific ideas you expect when you read my topic sentence?

Are there any abstract words in my topic sentence?

What else will help you understand my main idea?

Now, compare your classmate's responses and your own list of details. Should you add some ideas for support to your list? Are your details specific and concrete?

Write Your First Draft

Write a first draft without worrying about mechanics or correctness. Try to explain your main idea with plenty of specific and concrete detail. Return to your pre-writing activities—your writing journal and your list of ideas—anytime you need to.

Revise Your Paragraph

When you are finished, edit your paragraph support. Eliminate all information that is either equally general or more general than your topic sentence. Integrate into your support as much concrete detail as you can. Make a photocopy of your paragraph to bring to class.

Trade paragraphs with your partner. Edit each other's paragraphs as you did the sample paragraph. Put your marks on the extra copy so that the writer can decide what changes to make to the original. Consider your partner's feedback. If you are unsure whether or how to edit your composition, consult with your instructor. When you are satisfied with your paragraph, make a final copy to turn in to your instructor.

4

Young Minds

Courtesy of Jim and Tina Michaels

"The hand that rocks the cradle rules the world."

—William Ross Wallace

Think about the Topic

- How do children learn?
- How do relationships with adults affect young children?
- What does the quote mean to you?

Reading 1: Building Baby's Brain: The Basics

In Your Writing Journal

Write this question at the top of a new page in your writing journal. Then write an answer based on your own knowledge and experience. Write as much as you can. Save your writing journal so you can add to it later.

What do young children, infancy to age three, need?

Before You Read...

Discuss with Your Classmates

- What do you know about how babies learn?
- Is genetics (heredity) or environment more important in a baby's early development?
- What effect does a parent or caregiver have on a child's intelligence?
- Make a guess about the meaning of the title "Building Baby's Brain."

Consider This Background Information

- Babies are born with a need and desire to learn.
- At birth, babies can distinguish the smell and voices of their mothers from those of other people.
- Babies are born with the ability to learn any language, but by six months of age, a baby's brain only recognizes the sounds of the language it hears.
- The physical structure of a baby's brain can be changed.
- If an infant's body grew at the same rate as the brain grows, his or her weight would increase from 8.5 pounds at birth to 170 pounds at one month.
- Dr. Diane Bales is a professor and human development specialist. She creates programs to help parents and caregivers understand how young children develop and how to provide positive experiences in early childhood. One of her areas of expertise is early brain development. "Building Baby's Brain" is from her series "Better Brains for Babies."

Visit Your Writing Journal

What new ideas from your discussion can you add to your writing journal?

Step 1: Read for the Main Idea

First, read the selection quickly. Read it from beginning to end, and try to under-stand the writer's main idea and a few supporting ideas. Notice that some AWL words for vocabulary study are underlined. You should also underline any other words that are unfamiliar to you. Don't stop reading to look them up. Complete the outline at the end of the selection.

Building Baby's Brain: The Basics

Diane Bales, Professor and Human Development Specialist,
Cooperative Extension Service, the University of Georgia

marginalia

The early years are critical for later life. For years, scien-tists have known that what happens—or doesn't happen—during the first few years makes a big difference in a child's later life. Babies who do not get enough love and attention in infancy are less likely to be well-adjusted adults. Scientists recently have learned even more about how important the early years can be.

Wiring the Brain

A baby is born with more than 100 billion brain cells. Some of these cells are already connected to other cells at birth. These connections <u>regulate</u> the heartbeat and breath-ing, control reflexes, and regulate other <u>functions</u> needed to survive. But much of the brain's wiring does not happen until after birth. In the first months and years of life, brain cells form connections in many parts of the brain. These connec-tions are the <u>complex</u> circuits that shape our thinking, feel-ings, and behaviors.

During these early years, the brain cells make many more connections than the baby will use. The developing brain is a little like a fertile garden. When we plant a garden, we want the crops that we planted to grow and thrive. But when weeds start to grow, there is less room for our crops. By weeding out the plants we don't want, we allow more room for our crops to grow. The brain has a <u>similar</u> "weeding" process. By about age three, the brain cells have made many more connections than the child will ever need, but the brain is also efficient at weeding out the connections. It keeps track of the connections that the baby uses most. In time, the brain gets rid of the connections that it does not use regularly. The least-used connections are weeded out so that the most-used ones have more room to grow.

The Importance of Experience

From the moment a baby is born, every experience taken in by the five senses (hearing, seeing, touching, feeling, tasting) helps build the connections that guide development. No two brains are alike! Each child develops connections to deal with his or her experiences. For example, a hearing child makes many connections related to oral language. The brain of a deaf child does not get the experience needed to make those connections. A child who learns to play baseball will make certain connections that a child who never plays ball will not make.

The kind of care a child receives plays a big role in how the brain chooses to wire itself. Parents who talk and read to their babies are helping them develop important language connections. Parents who respond sensitively to their baby's cries are building the emotional connections that lead to healthier relationships.

What Can You Do?

Parents and other caregivers can help nurture <u>positive</u> brain development. Here are some of the most important ways you can help your baby's brain develop:

- *Remember that brain development begins before birth.* Nutrition makes a big difference in brain development even before the baby is born. Pregnant women should eat nutritious foods, avoid alcohol and other drugs, and have regular prenatal care to help <u>ensure</u> that their babies are born healthy.

■ *Make sure your baby's world is safe and <u>secure</u>.* Remove any safety hazards from the environment. Respond lovingly and <u>consistently</u> to your baby's cries. Give the baby attention. A baby feels <u>stress</u> when the environment is dangerous or when caregivers do not respond to him. Stress can slow brain development.

■ *Talk to your baby.* When the baby makes a sound, repeat it. Smile at the baby. Talk about the things you're doing together. Interacting face-to-face builds the brain connections needed for both language skills and a healthy emotional <u>bond</u>.

■ *Start reading aloud early.* Hearing adults read helps the brain develop language connections. It also gives parents and babies a chance to spend time together. <u>Furthermore</u>, reading aloud helps your baby build a lifelong love of books.

■ *Choose high-quality child care.* To ensure healthy development, babies need sensitive, loving care and stimulating experiences. Choose a child-care provider who will interact warmly with your baby one-on-one. Look for a safe and clean environment, a provider who understands how children grow and develop, and a rich variety of age-<u>appropriate</u> toys.

Finally, it is important to get information and help when you have questions about your baby's development. Ask your doctor questions. Have a librarian recommend good books on child development. Many communities in the United States have Extension Service offices that offer help. The information and help you receive can change your child's entire life. The early years of a baby's life only happen once, but those years last forever.

Based on your first reading, complete this outline:

The topic: _____

Write a word or phrase.

The main idea: _____

Write a complete sentence that tells the main idea.

_____

Some supporting ideas: _____

Write a different phrase or sentence on each line.

_____

_____

Do the supporting ideas help prove the main idea?

Step 2: Read for New Words

Return to Appendix A to review vocabulary strategies.

AWL Words to Know

These AWL words in order of appearance are underlined in the reading selection. Add them to your vocabulary journal.

regulate	similar	secure	bond
function	positive	consistently	furthermore
complex	ensure	stress	appropriate

Next, add any unfamiliar words that you underlined in Reading 1.

Follow these steps to complete your vocabulary journal:

1. Write the word and the sentence in the reading containing the word.

2. Note what part of speech the word should be based on its place in the sentence.

3. Guess the meaning of the word based on the sentence's meaning and the main idea of the reading selection.

4. Discuss your guess with your instructor and classmates, and confirm your guess by looking up the word up in the dictionary. Add any notes that will help you remember the meaning of the word.

5. Use the word in your own original sentence.

6. Gloss the reading selection before reading it a second time.

Step 3: Read for Answers

Reread Reading 1, and add marginalia in the wide right-hand margin. Then return to the reading to find the information that you need to complete this exercise. Prepare to discuss your answers.

1. What happens to a baby's brain during the first year of life?

2. What happens to connections in the brain that are not used?

3. A **simile** is a comparison of two different things using the word *like*. For example, *the stars are like diamonds in the sky*. Diane Bales uses a simile when she discusses the development of a baby's brain. To what does she compare a baby's brain?

Step 4: Read between the Lines

Do you think the writer of Reading 1 would agree or disagree with these statements? Return to the reading to discover the writer's opinion, and then circle A for agree or D for disagree. Prepare to give reasons for your answers. Remember to think about the <u>writer's opinion</u>, not your own opinion.

1. Brain development is completely determined by genetics.   A   D

2. Parents can influence their child's brain development.   A   D

3. Caregivers other than parents can also influence brain development. A   D

4. A professional writer's brain connections are different from a   A   D
   professional musician's.

5. Learning begins when a child enters school.   A   D

6. Babies need expensive toys to ensure brain development.   A   D

Step 5: Respond to the Reading

Reflect on your own knowledge and experience, and answer the questions. Remember to think about <u>your own opinions</u>. Be ready to discuss your answers.

1. What questions would you like to ask Diane Bales about brain development in young children?

2. Think about your own skills. Are you athletic? Good at languages? Musical? What can you remember about your early life that might have contributed to your skills as an adult?

3. Think back to the opening quote of this chapter: "The hand that rocks the cradle rules the world." Explain its meaning and rewrite the quote in your own words.

Return to Your Writing Journal

Return to your writing journal, and review your response to the opening question for Reading 1. What new ideas and opinions do you have now? How have your ideas about early learning changed? What information about young children surprised you? Review your answers in Step 5: Respond to the Reading. Add your new thoughts to your response. Write as much as you can.

Reading 2: Fathers Provide Bridge over the River of Goo

In Your Writing Journal

Write the question at the top of a new page in your writing journal. Then write an answer based on your own knowledge and experience. Write as much as you can. Save your writing journal so you can add to it later.

What role do fathers play in their children's upbringing?

Before You Read...

Discuss with Your Classmates

- Adolescence, or the teenage years, is considered a difficult time period in a person's life. Is this true universally (in all cultures)? Is this true in your native culture?

- Why is adolescence a difficult time period in a person's life?

- What is self-esteem?

- How are the problems of adolescent girls different from the problems of adolescent boys?

- How is the father-daughter relationship different from the mother-daughter relationship?

- Describe the ideal father-daughter relationship.

Consider This Background Information

- Adolescence is a time of great change—physically, socially, emotionally, and intellectually.

- Teenagers listen to and associate with their friends more than their parents or other adults.

- Self-esteem is a person's feelings of respect for himself or herself and his or her feeling of self-pride.

- Studies of father-daughter relationships show that:
  - a good father-daughter relationship improves a woman's self-esteem.
  - girls want to have more time with their fathers.
  - the time spent with one another consists of shared activities and doing things rather than having intimate conversations.
  - fathers want to keep their daughters away from the dangers of the world and negative peer and romantic relationships.

Visit Your Writing Journal

What new ideas from your discussion can you add to your writing journal?

Step 1: Read for the Main Idea

First, read the selection quickly. Read it from beginning to end, and try to understand the writer's main idea and a few supporting ideas. Notice that some AWL words for vocabulary study are underlined. Underline any other words that are unfamiliar to you. Don't stop reading to look them up. Complete the outline at the end of the selection.

Journalist Leonard Pitts described the changes in girls when they reach adolescence. Pitts calls this difficult time of change "the River of Goo." Kathleen Parker, a journalist for the Tribune Media Service, wrote a response to Pitts' article. In this excerpt from her response, Parker talks about the importance of her father in her life.

Fathers Provide Bridge over the River of Goo

marginalia

No single influence is more important to a girl's self-esteem and her future than her father. Studies support this <u>notion</u>, including a recent one out of England by a researcher named Adrienne Katz. In her Can-Do Girls report <u>published</u> last year, Katz found that girls with the highest self-esteem and self-confidence had a strong father-daughter relationship.

John Snarey, in his book *How Fathers Care for the Next Generation: A Four-<u>Decade</u> Study,* found that fathers who supported their daughters' <u>physical</u>-athletic and social-emotional development <u>contributed</u> greatly to their adult educational and <u>occupational</u> success.

But my belief in the importance of fathers isn't scientific; it's personal. My father reared me from the time I was three, after my mother died. Here's what I know about fathers and daughters and the River of Goo.

My father didn't rear me to be a girl. He just reared me. He clocked me when I ran and praised me when I beat the neighborhood boys. He rarely told me I was pretty, even though every father thinks his daughter is. What I remember most is his telling me: "Looks aren't important. It's what you do that matters. Now go read a book."

When I asked a word's meaning, he always said, "Look it up." He never would tell me himself. To look it up was to learn it.

"Do everything you can," he said. "Go everywhere, experience everything." I left home at 17 and never went home again except to visit.

"Think for yourself," he said. Once I was a teen, my father never told me what I could or couldn't do. He told me his opinion, then dropped the burden of decision into my lap. Of course, I always did what he wanted. How could I not? He was right.

"Be slow to know," he said about boys. "Don't give yourself away, hold your cards close, keep yourself to yourself." He taught me to play poker so I could keep a straight face, and to shoot a gun, so I could if I had to.

He took me on trips to learn to dine and dance. "Be a good listener," he said. "That's all a man wants. Leave the first time he raises a hand. He'll do it again."

"Peel the potatoes, Catalina," he said almost every night. He was Irish; I'm a master potato peeler. While I peeled, he cooked dinner, and we talked about whatever came to mind. Can I do this? Should I do that?

He said, "You can do anything."

Funny, I believed him.

I can't speak to the value of mothers to their daughters. I don't recommend growing up without one. But I can't fathom growing up without a father. They speak differently to daughters than mothers do. They allow you to take risks; they teach you your worth in the presence of men. They say things like "Chin up, Catalina. Keep your eye on the ball."

I'm not worried about Pitts' daughter. She has Leonard. But I do worry about the many girls growing up without fathers, owing to divorce, divisive custody arrangements or the misguided decisions of some women to become single mothers. I would wager that behind most women who successfully crossed the River of Goo was a man, and his name was Dad.

Source: Kathleen Parker, *The Orlando Sentinel,* August 16, 1998.

Based on your first reading, complete this outline:

The topic: _____

Write a word or phrase.

The main idea: _____

Write a complete sentence that states the main idea.

_____

Some supporting ideas: _____

Write a different phrase or sentence on each line.

_____

_____

Do the supporting ideas help prove the main idea?

Step 2: Read for New Words

Return to Appendix A to review vocabulary-building strategies.

AWL Words to Know

These AWL words in order of appearance are underlined in the reading selection. Add them to your vocabulary journal.

notion	decade	contributed
published	physical	occupational

Add any unfamiliar words that you underlined in Reading 2.

Follow these steps to complete your vocabulary journal.

1. Write the word and the sentence in the reading containing the word.
2. Note what part of speech the word should be based on its place in the sentence.
3. Guess the meaning of the word based on the sentence's meaning and the main idea of the reading selection.
4. Discuss your guess with your instructor and classmates, and confirm your guess by looking up the word in the dictionary. Add any notes that will help you remember the meaning of the word.
5. Use the word in your own original sentence.
6. Gloss the reading selection before reading it a second time.

Step 3: Read for Answers

Reread Reading 2, and add marginalia in the wide right-hand margin. Then return to the reading to find the information that you need to complete this exercise. Prepare to discuss your answers.

1. Why did Kathleen Parker have only one parent?

2. According to Parker, what is most important for a girl's self-esteem and future success?

3. What is the basis for her belief?

4. Write two examples of activities Parker and her father did together.
   a.

   b.

5. Write examples of advice Parker received from her father and how she used his advice.

<u>Father's advice</u>	<u>His daughter's actions</u>
go everywhere you can	*she left home at age 17*

Step 4: Read between the Lines

When you read between the lines, you understand meanings and information that are not directly stated. Kathleen Parker suggests many things about herself, her father, and their relationship without stating them. When you figure out her unstated meanings, you are making inferences or inferring.

Based on Kathleen Parker's description of her father-daughter relationship, would these statements most likely be true or false? Prepare to give reasons for your answers.

1. Parker's father influenced her decision to become a journalist.
   probably true   probably false

2. Parker listened to her father's advice before making a decision.
   probably true   probably false

3. Parker's father tried to play the role of a mother after his wife died.
   probably true   probably false

4. Parker has a lot of self-confidence.
   probably true   probably false

5. Being reared by only a father influenced Parker's relationships with men.
   probably true   probably false

6. Parker's father is proud of his daughter.
   probably true   probably false

Step 5: Respond to the Reading

Reflect on your own knowledge and experience, and answer the questions. Remember to think about <u>your own opinions</u>. Be ready to discuss your answers.

1. How has your father influenced you? How has your mother?

2. What is the greatest contribution a father can make to a daughter's life?

3. What is the greatest contribution a mother can make to a son's life?

Return to Your Writing Journal

Return to your writing journal, and review your response to the opening question for Reading 2. What new ideas and opinions do you have now? Do you think Kathleen Parker's father is a typical American father? How do you think a father-daughter relationship is different from a father-son relationship? What are the characteristics of a good parent-child relationship? Add your new thoughts to your response. Write as much as you can.

Writing Workshop: Paragraph Unity

In Chapters 1–3, you have learned about achieving your purpose as writer: helping the reader understand what are you are saying in your paragraph. So far you have learned to tell your reader your topic and your attitude about it and to provide support for your attitude. You know to develop your paragraph with concrete and specific support. There are two more characteristics of a well-written paragraph. These are **unity** and **coherence**. This Writing Workshop is about paragraph unity.

What Is Paragraph Unity?

Every well-written paragraph has **unity.** An academic paragraph develops just **one main idea** that is expressed in the topic sentence. When every sentence of a paragraph relates to a clearly stated main idea, a paragraph has **unity**. Unity means that all the sentences in the paragraph illustrate or explain the main idea. A unified paragraph should not include any sentences that do not offer support for the main idea. Such sentences are irrelevant or "off-topic." You can think of a paragraph as a highway map. Each sentence is a street or a turn on your map, but one wrong turn will prevent you from reaching your destination. To arrive at your destination, a wrong turn must be avoided. This is true for irrelevant sentences in a paragraph. Giving the reader a wrong direction will interfere with meaning.

Return to Reading 1, "Building Baby's Brain," and look at paragraph 3 on pages 78 and 79. The first sentence is the topic sentence and alerts the reader to expect a discussion of the overproduction of brain cell connections in the early years of a child's life. Now look at each sentence and note how each further explains this idea. Notice that the writer uses a simile to help the reader's understanding. Furthermore, the writer explains the result of having more connections than the baby will use. This paragraph has unity because only one idea is discussed, and it is explained thoroughly.

Now return to Reading 2 and read Kathleen Parker's opening paragraph on page 85. Although this paragraph is short, it has unity. Her main idea is a father's importance for a girl's self-esteem. The support sentences each talk about studies that prove her main idea. The writer discusses one idea and supports that idea. Thus, it is a unified paragraph.

Writing Activity 1: Practice Revising for Unity

Cross out the irrelevant or "off-topic" sentences in each paragraph.

1. From conception until about the third birthday, the brain grows at an amazing speed. During pregnancy, 50,000 brain cells, called neurons, are formed per second. This means it is especially important for pregnant women to eat healthy food. By birth the brain has 100 billion neurons—all that it will ever have. Yet the brain is the least developed organ at birth. The parts of the brain are in place, but most of its neurons are unconnected. The baby's brain doubles in weight by age three. When a five-year-old child starts school, his or her brain has reached 90 percent of its adult size. There is no other time in a child's life during which so much brain growth takes place. *(Find one irrelevant sentence.)*

2. Adults make learning language easier for babies. Most adults naturally talk differently to babies than to adults. They talk more slowly, raise the pitch of their voices, and exaggerate the accents in words. These changes make it easier for babies to hear language and recognize the patterns of words. Even children as young as four years old make some of these changes in their speech when talking to a baby. Adults also tend to repeat words and phrases when they talk to babies. Repetition helps babies learn to understand speech and strengthens the language connections in the brain. Repetition also helps adults who are learning a new language, but they need more repetition than babies need. Babies with hearing problems do not get the language experience they need to learn language. *(Find three irrelevant sentences.)*

<u>Remember</u>: As a writer, you must help the reader understand exactly what you are saying in your paragraph. To do this, a single main idea, stated in the topic sentence, must be developed with specific and concrete support. Every sentence in your paragraph must contribute to the main idea and not be "off-topic."

Time to Write

In this paragraph you will once again work on improving the support for your main idea. In addition to using concrete and specific support, you must make sure that every sentence adds new support to your main idea. Your goal is to write a unified paragraph.

Start Your Paragraph

Now return to your writing journal, and read over your responses to the opening journal questions for Readings 1 and 2. Choose one response to develop in a paragraph. Identify the topic of your paragraph, and add a controlling idea. Write your topic sentence. You can modify your topic sentence as you are writing if the support you choose makes a change necessary.

Return to your writing journal to gather details that support your topic sentence. Make a list of details to include as support. Be sure each detail contributes to the one main idea of your paragraph.

Write Your First Draft

Write a first draft without worrying about mechanics or correctness. Try to explain your main idea with plenty of specific and concrete detail that is "on topic." Return to your pre-writing activities—your writing journal and your list of ideas—anytime you need to.

Edit and Revise Your Paragraph for Unity

When you are finished, edit your paragraph for unity. Eliminate any sentence that is not "on topic." Make a photocopy of your paragraph to bring to class.

Trade paragraphs with your partner. Edit each other's paragraph for unity. As you read your partner's paragraph, examine each sentence and ask yourself:

Is this sentence "on topic"?

How is this detail related to the main idea of the paragraph?

Mark any sentences that prevent the paragraph from being unified. Put your marks on the extra copy so that the writer can decide what changes to make to the original. Consider your partner's feedback. If you are unsure whether or how to edit your paragraph, consult with your instructor.

Write your final copy of your paragraph to turn in to your instructor.

5

Better Business for the Next Millennium

Courtesy of Ohio Historical Society

1914, Grandview Heights/Marble Cliff

"What helps people, helps business."
—Leo Burnett, American Marketing Expert

"Conducting your business in a socially responsible way is good business. It means that you can attract better employees and that customers will know what you stand for and like you for it."
—M. Anthony Burns, CEO of Ryder Systems

Think about the Topic

- What makes a business successful?
- What makes an employer a good employer?
- What makes an employee a good employee?

Reading 1: Mentofacturing: A Vision for American Industrial Excellence

In Your Writing Journal

Write this question at the top of a new page in your writing journal. Then write an answer based on your own knowledge and experience. Write as much as you can. Save your writing journal so you can add to it later.

Describe the kind of work situation and employer-employee relationship that can bring success to a company.

Before You Read...

Discuss with Your Classmates

- What was the most satisfying job you have held? Why was it satisfying?
- What was the least satisfying job you have held? Why wasn't it satisfying?
- In your opinion, what is the responsibility of the employee to the employer?
- What is the responsibility of the employer to the employee?
- When searching for a job, what criteria are most important to you?

Consider This Background Information

- Twenty five percent of U.S. workers have manufacturing jobs.
- Manufacturing is the process of changing raw materials into finished products.
- Manufacturing adds value to materials by increasing their usefulness.
- Manufacturing output can be measured according to the value added.
- There are 350,000 manufacturing establishments in the United States.
- Since the late 1700s, most industries have used mass production to maximize profits.
- In mass production, each worker has one specific job that he or she does repeatedly.
- In most cases, managers, not workers, make the important decisions about how the work is done.
- Each company has its own management style.

Visit Your Writing Journal

What new ideas from your discussion can you add to your writing journal?

Step 1: Read for the Main Idea

First, read the selection quickly. Read it from beginning to end, and try to understand the writer's main idea and a few supporting ideas. Notice that some AWL words for vocabulary study are underlined. Underline any other words that are unfamiliar to you. Don't stop reading to look them up. Complete the outline at the end of the selection.

Mentofacturing: A Vision for American Industrial Excellence

marginalia

To be world industrial leaders, America's basic industrial organizations must change from manufacturing organizations to "mentofacturing" organizations. Manufacturing means "making by hand." Mentofacturing means "making by mind." Organizations must emphasize learning, human development, risk-taking, and technology.

An example of an organization that has changed in this way is Chaparral Steel. This company has a <u>culture</u> based on its <u>founders'</u> values and beliefs. Chaparral Steel sees employees as "human <u>resources</u>" for development, not "<u>labor</u> costs." Chaparral Steel executives believe that human beings are basically good, energetic, creative, and trustworthy—able to do great things. With these beliefs, the company has <u>achieved</u> high product quality, low product cost, and good customer service.

Chaparral Steel produces medium-sized steel products (bars, beams, angles and other simple items) for sale to construction, auto, railroad, mobile home, defense, appliance, and other companies. The company began in 1975, with a <u>capacity</u> of 220,000 tons. Its current capacity is 1.5 million tons. Its employees increased from 235 to 934. Of these, 880 employees work directly with the steel-making process. Since 1986, the number

of employees has decreased 1–2 percent each year while production has increased 100,000 tons <u>annually</u>.

The reason for Chaparral's success may be the compa-
ny's value of <u>innovation</u> and technology. A traditional steel
mill needs several days to manufacture finished steel products. Chaparral Steel needs only a few hours. The company
depends on the employees who make the steel to think of
ways to speed up production. For example, Chaparral had a
production line that produced 3,000 feet of steel bars per minute. The employees wanted to run the production line faster,
but they had a problem with bars becoming airborne in the
process! After months of experiments and planning, they
discovered that if they split the bars in the middle of the process, they could produce two bars at 3,000 feet per minute.
Next, they produced four bars at 3,000 feet per minute. The
Japanese have bought the license to use this new technology.

The company culture of Chaparral Steel encourages
employees to participate in the company's success. The firm
sees workers as business partners. For example, Chaparral
formed a "Founder's Club," but this club is for all employees,
not just managers or executives. Also, the company has a "no
fault" absence policy. All employees are paid a salary, not an
hourly wage, and an employee can be absent for a good reason or no reason. Employees are seen as adults. Surprisingly,
the daily absence rate is less than one percent. In fact, even the
<u>design</u> of the Chaparral building encourages employee par-
ticipation. Everyone must walk through the Human Resource
Department twice a day to get to his or her locker. The executive offices are also located in the same building as the locker
rooms. Consequently, it is convenient for all employees to talk
with each other. The training <u>facility</u> for all employees is better equipped than the executives' boardroom. All production
and <u>maintenance</u> employees help supervisors define <u>goals</u>.
Furthermore, these employees decide how to reach these goals
and decide what materials they need.

marginalia

Chaparral's employees are able to participate in the success of the company because they are trained in a 3½-year program that is <u>registered</u> with the U.S. Department of Labor and the Texas State Technical Institute. Employees earn college credit while learning skills. They spend four hours per week in a classroom during this training. Furthermore, they are paid an additional $20.00 per week to cover extra costs. Their trainers are outside professionals and other Chaparral employees. In the U.S., this kind of training is usually provided only for managers. Only 20–30 percent of machine operators and craft workers receive job training. However, at Chaparral, more than 90 percent of employees are in continuing education. Chaparral even has an English professor who regularly teaches creative writing to employees.

Employees are also rewarded for the success of the company. Everyone is on salary, and 62 percent of the employees own company stock. No two people earn the same salary, and increases are given on each employee's anniversary, based upon his or her individual knowledge and performance. Employees' performance evaluation is not based upon job descriptions because Chaparral doesn't use job descriptions. Evaluations are based upon the employees' own goals.

Not surprising, Chaparral's turnover rate is less than 2 percent per quarter. However, the company receives between 150–160 applications each month. Applicants go through a six-week process, including three interviews, testing, and <u>orientation</u>. Chaparral looks for people who have the communication ability, energy and sincerity to become an active team member.

Chaparral Steel is one example of successful mentofacturing. This firm has found that its values of ability instead of <u>authority</u>, mindfulness instead of busy-ness, and unity instead of division are not just <u>revolutionary</u> ideas, but also good business.

Source: Adapted from Gordon E. Forward, Dennis E. Beach, David A. Gray, and James Campbell Quick, "Mentofacturing: A Vision for American Industrial Excellence," *The Academy of Management 5*, no. 3 (1991): 1.

Based on your first reading, complete this outline:

The topic: _____
Write a word or phrase.

The main idea: _____
Write a complete sentence that tells the main idea.

_____

Some supporting ideas: _____
Write a different phrase or sentence on each line.

_____

_____

Do the supporting ideas help prove the main idea?

Step 2: Read for New Words

Return to Appendix A to review vocabulary-building strategies.

AWL Words to Know

These AWL words in order of appearance are underlined in the reading selection. Add them to your vocabulary journal.

culture	achieved	design	registered
founder	capacity	facility	orientation
resources	annually	maintenance	authority
labor	innovation	goals	revolutionary

Next, add any unfamiliar words that you underlined in Reading 1.

Follow these steps to complete your vocabulary journal:

1. Write the word and the sentence in the reading containing the word.
2. Note what part of speech the word should be based on its place in the sentence.
3. Guess the meaning of the word based on the sentence's meaning and the main idea of the reading selection.
4. Discuss your guess with your instructor and classmates, and confirm your guess by looking up the word in the dictionary. Add any notes that will help you remember the meaning of the word.
5. Use the word in your own original sentence.
6. Gloss the reading selection before reading it a second time.

Step 3: Read for Answers

Reread Reading 1, and add marginalia in the wide right-hand margin. Then return to the reading to find the information that you need to complete this exercise. Prepare to discuss your answers.

1. What is mentofacturing?

2. How is mentofacturing different from manufacturing?

3. The founders of Chaparral Steel believed that its employees were "basically good, energetic, creative, and trustworthy." Because of this belief, Chaparral employees have unusual opportunities. Find three examples in the article of the employees' opportunities:
   a.

   b.

   c.

4. Chaparral Steel has been a successful company. Find evidence of the company's success in the article:
   a.

   b.

   c.

Step 4: Read between the Lines

Do you think the writer of Reading 1 would agree or disagree with these statements? Return to the reading to discover the writer's opinion, and then circle A for agree or D for disagree. Prepare to give reasons for your answers. Remember to think about the writer's opinion, not your own opinion.

1. Manufacturing is as effective as mentofacturing.	A	D
2. Chaparral Steel is a typical U.S. company.	A	D
3. All employees of a company should have equal privileges.	A	D
4. All employees should help a company define its goals.	A	D

Step 5: Respond to the Reading

Reflect on your own knowledge and experience, and answer the questions. Remember to think about <u>your own opinions</u>. Be ready to discuss your answers.

1. The author believes that mentofacturing *must* replace manufacturing in American industry. Do you agree? Why or why not?

2. Chaparral receives about 160 employment applications each month. Why do you think so many people want to work for this company?

3. Chaparral selects employees who have good communication skills, a lot of energy, and are sincere. Write questions a Chaparral interviewer might ask in order to learn if an applicant has these qualities. (Example: To learn about an applicant's energy level, an interviewer might ask, "What are your favorite recreational activities?")

4. What information in the article is surprising to you?

5. What else would you like to know? Write three questions that the reading selection does not answer.

    a.

    b.

    c.

Return to Your Writing Journal

Return to your writing journal, and review your response to the opening question. What new ideas and opinions do you have now? Has your idea of a good employer-employee relationship changed? What are the characteristics of a good employer? What can an employee do to be the best possible employee? Add your new thoughts to your response. Write as much as you can.

Reading 2: Southwest Airlines' Rapid Climb

In Your Writing Journal

Write this question at the top of a new page in your writing journal. Then write an answer based on your own knowledge and experience. Write as much as you can. Save your writing journal so you can add to it later.

What are the characteristics of a successful business?

Before You Read...

Discuss with Your Classmates

- When you travel by airplane, what services do you expect the airline to provide?

- Can you remember an unpleasant experience with air travel? What went wrong?

- Can you remember a pleasant experience? What made the trip enjoyable?

- When you are planning to travel by airplane, how do you choose the airline you will fly with?

- What do you think is most necessary for an airline to be successful?

Consider This Background Information

- An airline is an organization of people, airplanes, equipment, and buildings for transporting people.

- In industrialized countries, city-to-city air travel is the fastest growing form of travel.

- The United States has more than 60 commercial airlines, carrying more than half of the world's passengers and cargo.

- Airlines travel in controlled air space on designated routes.

- In 1938 the Civil Aeronautics Board began to specify what routes airlines could fly and what prices they could charge for tickets.

- The Airline Deregulation Act of 1978 ended the Board's control.

- Most airlines earned a profit each year until the late 1970s.

- Higher fuel prices and fewer passengers caused many airlines to lose profit, and some went out of business.

- At the same time, Southwest Airlines was quickly growing to be one of the most profitable airlines in the world.

Visit Your Writing Journal

What new ideas from your discussion can you add to your writing journal?

Step 1: Read for the Main Idea

First, read the selection quickly. Read it from beginning to end, and try to understand the writer's main idea and a few supporting ideas. Notice that some AWL words for vocabulary study are underlined. Underline any other words that are unfamiliar to you. Don't stop reading to look them up. Complete the outline at the end of the selection.

Southwest Airlines' Rapid Climb

marginalia

Herbert Kelleher and Rollin King founded Southwest Airlines in March 1967. At that time the company offered flights inside Texas. The company couldn't offer flights between states because the airline industry was tightly controlled at that time. They wanted to start an airline that would offer low fares. They thought a lot of people wanted to fly but couldn't because the cost was too high. While other airlines were saying, "Only business people fly and somebody else is paying for their transportation . . . so whenever we get in financial trouble, we will increase our fares," Southwest decided to lower their fares. Kelleher and King also wanted Southwest to be a short-distance carrier. They were going to compete with the automobile, so it was very important for them to offer fares that were lower than the cost of driving an automobile. In fact, five or six years after they started their business, another airline, Braniff, was charging $62.00 for flights between Dallas and San Antonio, but Southwest was charging only $15.00. They also wanted people to be able to travel when they wanted to travel. So eventually they had 80 flights between Dallas and Houston per day! They believed that people's time was important, so their goal was to have 90 percent on-time performance, and by the late '80s, according to Department of Transportation <u>statistics</u>, they were number one in the industry in on-time performance. Next, they looked at total trip time, including time in the air, time getting to the airport, and time getting on the airplane, and decided to shorten it. They created quick ticketing machines that <u>issue</u> a ticket in 10 seconds. They decided that speedy baggage handling was important, and today they can deliver baggage from the airplane to the baggage claim area in only eight minutes. The airline has reserved seating, but not <u>assigned</u> seating. This means that customers have a seat on the airplane reserved, but they are not assigned a particular seat. Thus, there are good seats <u>available</u> for passengers who arrive early for departure. Finally, Kelleher and King decided it was important to lure caring employees who would provide cheerful service. Later, they did a survey on their airplanes, and passengers said that Southwest Airlines employees cared more for them than employees at any other airline on which they flew.

Has Southwest Airlines succeeded? Well, the company has grown from 3 aircraft to 144 aircraft; from providing service in 3 airports to 60 airports. Southwest Airlines has been profitable every year since 1973. Its net income at the end of 2004 was $313 million with a total operating <u>revenue</u> of $6.5 billion.

The company's climb to the top has been quick and steady. And it is still climbing.

Source: Adapted from Herbert D. Kelleher, "Southwest Airlines: Past, Present, and Future," *Executive Speeches* 3, 1988. *http://proquest.umi.com/*

Based on your first reading, complete this outline:

The topic: _____

Write a word or phrase.

The main idea: _____

Write a complete sentence that tells the main idea.

_____

Some supporting ideas: _____

Write a different phrase or sentence on each line.

_____

_____

Do the supporting ideas help prove the main idea?

Step 2: Read for New Words

Return to Appendix A to review vocabulary-building strategies.

AWL Words to Know

These AWL words in order of appearance are underlined in the reading selection. Add them to your vocabulary journal.

transportation	issue	available
statistics	assigned	revenues

Next, add any unfamiliar words that you underlined in Reading 2.

Follow these steps to complete your vocabulary journal:

1. Write the word and the sentence in the reading containing the word.
2. Note what part of speech the word should be based on its place in the sentence.
3. Guess the meaning of the word based on the sentence's meaning and the main idea of the reading selection.
4. Discuss your guess with your instructor and classmates, and confirm your guess by looking up the word up in the dictionary. Add any notes that will help you remember the meaning of the word.
5. Use the word in your own original sentence.
6. Gloss the reading selection before reading it a second time.

Step 3: Read for Answers

Reread Reading 2, and add marginalia in the wide right-hand margin. Then return to the reading to find the information that you need to complete this exercise. Prepare to discuss your answers.

1. Successful business owners realize that it is impossible to please everyone. It is essential to target a group of people as a market and determine how to meet the needs of that market. Whom did Southwest Airlines target as their market, and how did they set out to please them?

2. A company succeeds when it meets its goals. List the original goals of Southwest Airlines and the evidence of its success in achieving each.

Goals	Evidence of Success
Lower air fares	*$15.00 fare between Dallas and San Antonio*

3. What could owners of other small businesses learn from Southwest Airlines?

Step 4: Read between the Lines

Do you think the writer of Reading 2 would agree or disagree with these statements? Return to the reading to discover the writer's opinion, and then circle A for agree or D for disagree. Prepare to give reasons for your answers. Remember to think about the writer's opinion, not your own opinion.

1. Southwest should have restricted their business to flights inside Texas. A   D

2. It is best to offer as many flights as possible between two places.   A   D

3. Assigned seating is better for passengers.   A   D

4. Southwest will continue to be successful in the future.   A   D

Step 5: Respond to the Lines

Reflect on your own knowledge and experience, and answer the questions. Remember to think about <u>your own opinions</u>. Be ready to discuss your answers.

1. The last time you flew, which airline did you use? Why did you choose that airline?

2. Rate the service you received in each of these categories as poor (P), fair (F), or good (G). Explain your answers.

   _____ flight availability   _____ boarding   _____ refreshments

   _____ ticketing   _____ baggage   _____ punctuality of

   departure/arrival

   What other categories of airline performance can be rated?

3. Review Southwest's goals. What other goals should an airline have in order to ensure customer satisfaction?

Return to Your Writing Journal

Return to your writing journal, and review your response to the opening question for Reading 2. What new ideas and opinions do you have now? How do customers influence a business? What do you think this saying means: "The customer is always right"? What is your opinion of this saying? Add your new thoughts to your response. Write as much as you can.

Writing Workshop: Paragraph Coherence 1

You have learned to write a paragraph that has a topic and controlling idea, that is well-developed with specific and concrete support, and that is unified. **Coherence** is another characteristic of a well-written paragraph that helps make meaning clear to the reader. In this Writing Workshop you will practice using transition words to make your paragraph coherent.

What Is Paragraph Coherence?

A well-written paragraph has **coherence**. A paragraph is coherent when the ideas in the paragraph are clear and easy to follow. The reader can move easily from one idea to the next because the writer has shown connections and relationships within the paragraph. In other words, the paragraph has a smooth flow.

One way the writer creates coherence is by connecting sentences with **transition words.** *On the other hand, in fact, consequently, for example, therefore, in addition, also, furthermore, in conclusion,* and *finally* are just a few of the transition words writers often use. Like signs on an interstate highway, transition words give the reader information about what is coming next in the paragraph. This helps the reader understand the relationships between the writer's ideas.

Consider this paragraph.

Studying at a small private college has both advantages and disadvantages. One advantage is the personal attention students receive. The average class size at my college is only 15. Everyone gets the chance to ask the professor questions. It is easy to find your way from one class to another. It is also very easy to make new friends at a small private college. There are fewer student activities to choose from. Many of my friends travel to the larger university nearby for parties and student meetings. Small private colleges aren't the best choice for everyone, but I am satisfied with my selection.

Now read the same paragraph with transitions. When transitions are added, the paragraph has a smooth flow. It is easier to follow.

Studying at a small private college has both advantages and disadvantages. One advantage is the personal attention students receive. **For example,** the average class size at my college is only 15. **Therefore,** everyone gets the chance to ask the professor questions. **In addition,** it is easy to find your way from one class to another. It is also very easy to make new friends at a small private college. **On the other hand,** there are fewer student activities to choose from.

In fact, many of my friends travel to the larger university nearby for parties and student meetings. **In conclusion,** small private colleges aren't the best choice for everyone, but I am satisfied with my selection.

The transitions in the second paragraph show the reader the relationships among the ideas in the paragraph. These transitions hold the paragraph together and give it a smooth flow. Notice that there are not transitions between each and every sentence, but there are enough transitions to connect the ideas in the paragraph.

Writing Activity 1: Understanding Transitions

1. Write and discuss the meaning of each transition used in the paragraph.
   a. *for example*

   b. *therefore*

   c. *in addition*

   d. *on the other hand*

   e. *in fact*

   f. *in conclusion*

2. Now look at paragraph 5 of Reading 1, "Mentofacturing: A Vision for American Industrial Excellence" (page 97).

The company culture of Chaparral Steel encourages employees to participate in the company's success. The firm sees workers as business partners. For example, Chaparral formed a "Founder's Club," but this club is for all employees, not just managers or executives. Also, the company has a "no fault" absence policy. All employees are paid a salary, not an hourly wage, and an employee can be absent for a good reason or no reason. Employees are seen as adults. Surprisingly, the daily absence rate is less than one percent. In fact, even the design of the Chaparral building encourages employee participation. Everyone must walk through the Human Resource Department twice a day to get to his or her locker. The executive offices are also located in the same building as the locker rooms. Consequently, it is convenient for all employees to talk with each other. The training facility for all employees is better equipped than the executives' boardroom. All production and maintenance employees help supervisors define goals. Furthermore, these employees decide how to reach these goals and decide what materials they need.

Underline the five transitions used in this paragraph. Write and discuss the meaning of each transition listed.

a. *for example:*

b. *also:*

c. *in fact:*

d. *consequently:*

e. *furthermore:*

Writing Activity 2: Practice Revising for Coherence by Using Transitions

This paragraph needs transitions. Add appropriate transitions from the list.

also	consequently	furthermore
for example	therefore	in addition
on the other hand	in fact	in conclusion

An ethical company must be fair to its employees. It must pay employees a fair wage. An ethical company will provide benefits for its employees. It will provide insurance and paid medical leave. It must provide a healthy working environment. The working environment should be clean and free of hazards. Managers must make all policies and procedures clear. There will be fewer misunderstandings between employees and managers. When a company is fair to its employees, it is more likely to succeed in business.

<u>Remember</u>: As a writer, you must help the reader understand exactly what you are saying in your paragraph. Your ideas will be clearer if your paragraph has coherence. A coherent paragraph is one that is easy to follow. Adding transitions to show connections and relationships between ideas will give your paragraph coherence.

Time to Write

In this paragraph, you will work on making your paragraph easy to follow and understand. To do this, use transitions to show connections and relationships. Transitions are not necessary between each and every sentence, but there must be enough to give your paragraph a smooth flow. Your goal is to write a coherent paragraph.

Start Your Paragraph

Now return to your writing journal, and read over your responses to the opening journal questions for Readings 1 and 2. Choose one response to develop in a paragraph. Identify the topic of your paragraph and add a controlling idea. Write your topic sentence.

Return to your writing journal to gather details that support your topic sentence. Make a list of details to include as support. Does each detail help the reader understand your main idea? In other words, will your paragraph have unity? Before you add transitions to show connections, you should be sure your paragraph is about only one topic.

Write Your First Draft

Use your list of details and topic sentence to write your first draft. Don't worry about mechanics or correctness at this point. Remember to develop your main idea with plenty of concrete and specific detail. Return to your writing journal and list of details anytime you need to. Add transitions to connect your ideas and show relationships.

Edit and Revise Your Paragraph for Coherence

When you are finished, edit your paragraph for coherence. Is it easy for the reader to follow your ideas? Are there enough transitions? Make a photocopy of your paragraph to bring to class.

Trade paragraphs with your partner. Edit each other's paragraphs for coherence. Put your marks on the extra copy so that the writer can decide what changes to make to the original. Circle the transitions the writer has used. As you read your partner's paragraph, ask yourself:

- Does the paragraph have a smooth flow?
- Are the transitions appropriately placed in the paragraph?
- Would more transitions make the paragraph easier to follow?
- If so, where would additional transitions be helpful?
- Have transitions been overused, making the paragraph sound awkward?

Read your partner's paragraph aloud once with the suggested transitions and again without the suggested transitions. Discuss which transitions best create a smooth flow. Consider your partner's feedback. If you are unsure whether or how to edit your paragraph, consult with your instructor. Write your final copy of your paragraph to turn in to your instructor.

6

Science or Religion?

Charles Darwin 1809–1882

"Science without religion is lame, religion without science is blind."

—Albert Einstein

"Religions are many and diverse, but reason and goodness are one."

—*The Roycroft Dictionary and Book of Epigrams,* 1923

Think about the Topic

- How does religion influence a person's life?
- How has science affected world history?
- What do the quotes mean to you?

Reading 1: Kenneth Miller, Christian Evolutionist

In Your Writing Journal

Write this question at the top of a new page in your writing journal. Then write an answer based on your own knowledge and experience. Write as much as you can. Save your writing journal so you can add to it later.

Is it possible to believe in both creation and evolution? Why or why not?

Before You Read...

Discuss with Your Classmates

- Is it necessary to have proof before you believe something?
- How can scientists prove events that occurred before written history?
- What are your beliefs about how the world was created?
- What are your beliefs about how people first appeared on earth?
- What do you know about the theory of evolution? Share your ideas and opinions about evolution.

Consider This Background Information

- Creationism (also called Intelligent Design) is a faith-based belief that the beginning of life is due to a divine creator.
- Evolutionism is the scientific study of the origins and development of life. Evolutionists claim that life evolved from a single living cell.
- Kenneth Miller is a professor at Brown University. He teaches molecular biology, cell biology, and biochemistry. He has given many presentations about evolution.
- Charles Darwin lived from 1809 to 1882.
- Darwin was one of the most influential scientists of the 19th century. Before he graduated from Cambridge University in England as a naturalist, Darwin had studied to become a physician and a minister. He did not complete either of these fields of study.
- Darwin is best known for developing the theory of evolution by natural selection and the publication of *On the Origin of Species* in 1859.

- Darwin's theory of evolution has caused many disputes, especially in educational settings.
- In 1925 John Scopes, a Tennessee high school teacher, was brought to trial for teaching evolution.

Visit Your Writing Journal

What new ideas from your discussion can you add to your writing journal?

Step 1: Read for the Main Idea

First, read the selection quickly. Read it from beginning to end, and try to understand the writer's main idea and a few supporting ideas. Notice that some AWL words for vocabulary study are underlined. Underline any other words that are unfamiliar to you. Don't stop reading to look them up. Complete the outline at the end of the selection.

Kenneth Miller, Christian Evolutionist

marginalia

In his book, *Finding Darwin's God* (2000), Kenneth Miller, professor of biology at Brown University and author, responds to the modern argument of evolutionism vs. creationism. For him, evolution is a fact, but he believes it is possible to believe in evolution and believe in God as Creator, too.

In his book, he responds to many criticisms of evolution, including the argument that any theory about the past is not scientific because it cannot be proven in a laboratory experiment. This argument states that there is no person who has watched evolution occur, so it cannot be accepted as fact. Miller replies that there is a scientific way to learn about the past, and the police use it every day. For instance, when a burglar pries open a window and climbs into a home to steal, he hopes that he will leave without anyone hearing or seeing him. However, even if no one sees or hears him, every one of his actions leaves something behind. First, there will be marks from his tools on the window. His feet will leave prints on the carpet. Also, the police may be able to gather a sample of his hair or blood or find his fingerprints in the house. And eventually the things he took may be found in the marketplace. Miller insists that we can learn about the past of the Earth and its living creatures by doing police work. The past always leaves something behind. He states, "Every atom of the earth's substance that is here in this instant will still be here a minute from now. It may change form or shape, it may move, it may even <u>undergo</u> a <u>chemical</u> reaction, but matter <u>persists</u>, and that means that the present always contains clues to the past."

As a scientist, Miller is a biologist and an evolutionist. As a Christian, Miller is a Roman Catholic. His students often <u>assume</u> that he is an atheist because some scientists believe that the theory of natural <u>selection</u> replaces God as <u>Creator</u>. Miller does not. When his students occasionally ask him if he believes in God, he always answers, "Yes." When they ask him, "What kind of God?" he tells them to read the last chapter of Darwin's *On the Origin of Species*. In this chapter Darwin expresses his amazement at the endless variety and interdependence of living creatures. He expresses wonder that "the Creator," through the process of evolution, <u>created</u> both wonderful and beautiful forms of life, and He is still creating them. Miller believes in the Christian God, Who, in his opinion, is also Darwin's God.

Based on your first reading, complete this outline:

The topic: _____

Write a word or phrase.

The main idea: _____

Write a complete sentence that tells the main idea.

_____

Some supporting ideas: _____

Write a different phrase or sentence on each line.

_____

_____

Do the supporting ideas help prove the main idea?

Step 2: Read for New Words

Return to Appendix A to review vocabulary-building strategies.

AWL Words to Know

These AWL words in order of appearance are underlined in the reading selection. Add them to your vocabulary journal.

evolution	undergo	assume	created
theory	chemical	selection	
instance	persists	Creator	

Next, add any unfamiliar words that you underlined in Reading 1.

Follow these steps to complete your vocabulary journal:

1. Write the word and the sentence in the reading containing the word.

2. Note what part of speech the word should be based on its place in the sentence.

3. Guess the meaning of the word based on the sentence's meaning and the main idea of the reading selection.

4. Discuss your guess with your instructor and classmates, and confirm your guess by looking up the word in the dictionary. Add any notes that will help you remember the meaning of the word.

5. Use the word in your own original sentence.

6. Gloss the reading selection before reading it a second time.

Step 3: Read for Answers

Reread Reading 1, and add marginalia in the wide right-hand margin. Then return to the reading to find the information that you need to complete this exercise. Prepare to discuss your answers.

1. What is Kenneth Miller's profession?

2. What is the purpose of his book, *Finding Darwin's God*?

3. What criticism of evolution is mentioned in the reading?

4. Explain this statement in your own words: ". . . matter persists, and that means that the present always contains clues to the past."

5. Why do Miller's students often assume that he is an atheist?

6. In the last chapter of *On the Origin of Species,* which Miller mentions, about what does Darwin express "amazement and wonder"?

Step 4: Read between the Lines

Do you think the writer of this selection would agree or disagree with these statements? Return to the reading to discover the writer's opinion, and circle A for agree or D for disagree. Prepare to give reasons for your answers. Remember to think about the <u>writer's opinion</u>, not your own opinion.

1. Miller believes God created us.	A	D
2. Miller believes evolution created us.	A	D
3. Police work is scientific.	A	D
4. Science is more important than religion.	A	D

Step 5: Respond to the Reading

Reflect on your own knowledge and experience, and answer the questions. Remember to think about <u>your own opinions</u>. Be ready to discuss your answers.

1. In your opinion, is it possible to believe in God as Creator and accept the theory of evolution as fact? Why? Why not?

2. Give examples of what you find most amazing and wonderful in the natural world. Describe each example.

3. Can you think of any other scientific theories that are unacceptable to religious believers?

Return to Your Writing Journal

Return to your writing journal, and review your response to the opening question for Reading 1. What new ideas and opinions do you have now? How have your ideas about believing in both creationism and evolution changed? If you were a scientist, how would you deal with this question? Add your new thoughts to your response. Write as much as you can.

Reading 2: Dyson Honored with Templeton Prize

In Your Writing Journal

Write this question at the top of a new page in your writing journal. Then write an answer based on your own knowledge and experience. Write as much as you can. Save your writing journal so you can add to it later.

What can scientists and religious leaders learn from each other?

Before You Read...

Discuss with Your Classmates

- What is the relationship between science and religion?
- On what subjects do science and religion agree?
- On what subjects do science and religion disagree?
- What beliefs are common among many religions?
- How are wealth, science, and technology related?
- What is the impact of religion on science in your native country?

Consider This Background Information

- Sir John Templeton instituted the Templeton Prize in 1972.
- The Templeton Prize recognizes outstanding work connecting the sciences and all religions.
- Sir John Templeton became very wealthy as the founder of Templeton Growth Fund and Templeton World Fund. After selling his company, he became a full-time philanthropist, someone who donates money for the benefit of others.
- He uses his personal wealth to support hundreds of programs worldwide in the areas of science and religion, spirituality and health, character development, and the benefits of freedom and free competition.
- Freeman Dyson is a physicist and a mathematician. He was a professor at Princeton University in New Jersey.
- He has lectured all over the world, and he has written several books.
- One of his well-known books is *The Sun, the Genome and the Internet*. In this book he discusses how modern technology can help both rich and poor people.

Visit Your Writing Journal

What new ideas from your discussion can you add to your writing journal?

Step 1: Read for the Main Idea

First, read the selection quickly. Read it from beginning to end, and try to understand the writer's main idea and a few supporting ideas. Notice that some AWL words for vocabulary study are underlined. Underline any other words that are unfamiliar to you. Don't stop reading to look them up. Complete the outline at the end of the selection.

Dyson Honored with Templeton Prize

marginalia

New York—March 16, 2000

Freeman J. Dyson, a respected physicist who has asked people to bring together technology and social justice, has won the Templeton Prize for Progress in Religion. After receiving the award, Dyson responded with a statement to both modern scientists and theologians: "Don't imagine that our latest ideas about the Big Bang or the human genome have solved the mysteries of the universe or the mysteries of life. Four hundred years ago Sir Francis Bacon prayed: 'Humbly we pray that this mind always be in us and that through our hands and the hands of others, You will give people new mercies...' That is still a good prayer for all of us as we begin the 21st century."

According to Dyson, science and religion are two windows to the same universe, two ways to understand why we are here. Both views are one-sided; neither is complete, and neither one should take total control and claim to be perfect. Dyson added, "In the little town of Princeton, NJ, where I live, we have more than 20 churches and at least one synagogue, providing different forms of worship and belief for different kinds of people. They do more than any other organizations in the town to hold the community together. Within this community of people, held together by religious traditions of human brotherhood and sharing of burdens, a smaller community of scientists also flourishes." Dyson emphasizes that the most important question of our time is how to make sure that scientific discoveries bring <u>benefits</u> to everybody rather than make the rich richer and the poor poorer. Dyson hopes that technology—guided by ethics—will lift up poor countries—and poor people in rich countries and "give them a chance of a decent life." Dyson calls for scientists and business leaders to join with <u>environmentalists</u> and religious organizations to give political importance to ethics.

Source: from John Brockman and Freeman Dyson, "EDGE 68—May 16, 2000," Edge. *www.edge.org/documents/archive/edge68.html*

Based on your first reading, complete this outline:

The topic: _____

Write a word or phrase

The main idea: _____

Write a complete sentence that tells the main idea.

_____

Some supporting ideas: _____

Write a different phrase or sentence on each line.

_____

_____

Do the supporting ideas help prove the main idea?

Step 2: Read for New Words

Return to Appendix A to review vocabulary-building strategies.

AWL Words to Know

These AWL words in order of appearance are underlined in the reading selection. Add them to your vocabulary journal.

community	emphasizes	environmentalists
traditions	benefits	

Next, add any unfamiliar words that you underlined in Reading 2.

Follow these steps to complete your vocabulary journal:

1. Write the word and the sentence in the reading containing the word.
2. Note what part of speech the word should be based on its place in the sentence.
3. Guess the meaning of the word based on the sentence's meaning and the main idea of the reading selection.
4. Discuss your guess with your instructor and classmates, and confirm your guess by looking up the word up in the dictionary. Add any notes that will help you remember the meaning of the word.
5. Use the word in your own original sentence.
6. Gloss the reading selection before reading it a second time.

Step 3: Read for Answers

Reread Reading 2, and add marginalia in the wide right-hand margin. Then return to the reading to find the information that you need to complete this exercise. Prepare to discuss your answers.

1. Why did Dyson win the Templeton Prize?

2. What is Dyson asking for in the words of Bacon's prayer?

3. What does Dyson say is true about both science and religion?

4. According to Dyson, what is the most important question of our time?

5. What is his hope for the future?

Step 4: Read between the Lines

Would Freeman Dyson agree or disagree with these statements? Return to the reading to discover his opinions, and then circle A for agree or D for disagree. Prepare to give reasons for your answers. Remember to think about <u>Dyson's opinion</u>, not your own opinion.

1. Many people are too confident in the ability of science to solve problems.   A   D

2. What we do is more important than what we know.   A   D

3. A person cannot be both scientific and religious.   A   D

4. Technology is all that poor countries need.   A   D

Step 5: Respond to the Reading

Reflect on your own knowledge and experience, and answer the questions. Remember to think about <u>your own opinions</u>. Be ready to discuss your answers.

1. Who should decide which uses of technology are helpful and which are harmful?

2. Give examples of technology that, in your opinion, are helpful, harmful, and neutral (neither helpful nor harmful).

<u>Helpful</u>   <u>Harmful</u>   <u>Neutral</u>

Return to Your Writing Journal

Return to your writing journal, and review your response to the opening question for Reading 2. What new ideas and opinions do you have now? What examples can you give of science and religion as partners? How can scientists and religious leaders help each other? What situations in less-developed countries could be improved by a science-religion partnership? Add your new thoughts to your response. Write as much as you can.

Writing Workshop: Paragraph Coherence 2

You have learned to achieve coherence by using transitions to make it easier for a reader to follow your ideas. Another way to a achieve coherence is to arrange your sentences in a logical order. In this Writing Workshop you will practice using logical sentence order to make your paragraph coherent.

Paragraph Organization and Coherence

As you read in Chapter 5, **transitions** are like signs on an interstate highway because they give the reader information about what is coming next. But what would happen if the signs were in the wrong order? Using logical order means that ideas are arranged in an order that makes sense to the reader. The way sentences are arranged is called the **organizational pattern** of the paragraph. Every language organizes ideas differently. What is logical in one language is often not logical in another language. Knowing organizational patterns used in English will help you become a better writer and reader. Two common organizational patterns are **list order** and **time order**. Arranging ideas in a logical order in list or time order is another way to create a smooth flow. In addition to an easy-to-follow order, special transitions for list or time organization can be used.

List Order Organization

In list order organization, the writer gives a list of details to support the main idea of the paragraph. These details are usually reasons or examples that are often explained in the order of importance. Each detail is explained separately and completely before the writer moves on to the next detail. Often, but not always, a transition lets the reader know that a new detail is about to be discussed. Some of the transitions used in list order paragraphs are:

first	next	also	for instance
second	another	finally	for example
third	the other	in addition	furthermore

Now look at the excerpt from paragraph two in Reading 1, pages 115–16. In this paragraph, the writer uses an example to explain ways we can learn about the past from evidence left behind. The example is then explained in list order.

This argument states that there is no person who has watched evolution occur, so it cannot be accepted as fact. Miller replies that there is a scientific way to learn about the past, and the police use it every day. For instance, when a burglar pries open a window and climbs into a home to steal, he hopes that he will leave without anyone hearing or seeing him. However, even if no one sees or hears him, every one of his actions leaves something behind. First, there will be marks from his tools on the window. His feet will leave prints on the carpet. Also, the police may be able to gather a sample of his hair or blood or find his fingerprints in the house. And eventually the things he took may be found in the marketplace.

Answer the questions about the excerpt.

1. Underline the transitions.

2. What transition is used to tell the reader that an example follows?

3. List the details the writer gives to explain the example. If a transition is used to introduce the detail, write it.

Transition   Detail

a. *first* _____   *marks from the burglar's tools* _____

b. _____   _____

c. _____   _____

d. _____   _____

e. _____   _____

Writing Activity 1: Practice Revising for Coherence by Using List Order

1. This paragraph has enough transition words, but the sentence order is not chronological. Revise the sentence order by writing a number in the blank before each sentence. Be sure that all of the sentences that explain a particular detail are kept together. (<u>Hint</u>: First find the topic sentence, which summarizes the paragraph's main idea, and label it with a 1.)

_____ Each family member's uniqueness is honored with special gifts, food, and activities.

_____ For example, we always have a soccer game on my brother's birthday, but my very musical grandmother's birthday is always celebrated with a family sing-a-long.

_____ In conclusion, I am grateful to have a large family because we have many birthday parties every year.

_____ It is a time when parents recall the special day their child was born.

_____ A birthday party is always a joyful celebration in my home.

_____ First, it is joyful because it commemorates the miracle of birth.

_____ Second, a birthday party celebrates the uniqueness of each family member.

2. This paragraph is difficult to understand because it is lacking both transition words and logical sentence order. First, revise the sentence order by writing a number in the blank before each sentence. Next, add a few transitions to improve the paragraph more. The first sentence has been numbered for you.

_____ He became especially interested in Jupiter and discovered its moons.

_____ After he built an even stronger telescope, he was able see Mercury, Venus, Mars, and Jupiter.

_____ He built a strong telescope and began to study the skies.

_____ With this strong telescope, he was able to see the surface of the moon, the heavenly body closest to the earth.

___1___ Galileo, an Italian scientist, studied the skies and made an important discovery.

_____ By studying the planets and the skies with his telescope, Galileo concluded that the sun, not the earth, was the center of the universe.

Time Order Organization

In time order organization, often called chronological organization, details are arranged according to the order in which they occurred. The writer tells the reader what happened first, second, next, and so on. Some of the transitions used in time order paragraphs are:

first	next	soon	eventually	before/after 2006
second	during the 1900s	later	finally	
third	then	after	in 2006	

Notice that *first, second, third,* and *next* are used in both time order and list order paragraphs. In list order paragraphs these transitions are used to tell the reader that a new detail is going to be discussed. In time order paragraphs these transitions show chronological order.

Writing Activity 2: Practice Revising for Coherence by Using Time Order

I. The sentences below make up one paragraph. This paragraph has enough transition words, but the sentences should be arranged in time order. Revise the sentence order by writing a number in the blank before each sentence. (<u>Hint</u>: First find the topic sentence, which summarizes the paragraph's main idea, and label it with a I.)

_____ Soon after the Church's order of 1616, Galileo was called to Rome and warned not to defend his scientific ideas about the universe.

_____ Finally, in 1992, more than 350 years later, the Catholic Church apologized for the trial of Galileo and this great conflict between science and religion.

_____ The trial of Galileo, a scientist and a man of strong religious beliefs, may be the most famous conflict between science and religion.

_____ Then, in 1633, Galileo was brought to trial and condemned for believing the sun, not the earth, was the center of the universe.

_____ As early as 1616 the Catholic Church issued an order saying the idea of the sun as the center of the universe was wrong and anyone holding this view could be tortured, imprisoned, and put to death.

_____ In 1632, he published a book comparing the ideas of the sun as the center of the universe and the earth as the center of the universe.

2. The sentences below make up one paragraph. It is difficult to understand because it is lacking both transition words and time order. First, revise the sentence order by writing a number in the blank before each sentence. (See the Hint on page 127.) Next, add a few transitions that show time order to improve the paragraph more.

_____ Study each topic thoroughly, and give extra attention to the most difficult topics.

_____ Find a comfortable place with good lighting and enough space for all of the course materials.

_____ Preparing for an exam requires planning and organization.

_____ Do a quick review of everything one last time before the exam.

_____ Gather all the books, notes, and other papers you will need.

_____ Look over all of the study topics quickly to decide which topics will need extra attention.

Remember: As a writer, you must help the reader understand exactly what you are saying in your paragraph. Your ideas will be clearer if your sentences are arranged in a logical order. Transitions will help readers understand how your paragraph is organized and make it easy to follow.

Time to Write

In this paragraph, you will again work on making your paragraph coherent—easy to follow and understand. To do this, pay careful attention to the order of sentences. Add time or list transitions to help the reader understand the organization.

Start Your Paragraph

Now return to your writing journal, and read over your responses to the opening journal questions for Readings 1 and 2. Choose one response to develop in a paragraph. Identify the topic of your paragraph, and add a controlling idea. Write your topic sentence.

Return to your writing journal to gather details that support your topic sentence. Write each detail on a separate index card or small piece of paper. Arrange the index cards in the order you think is most logical. Try a couple of different arrangements. Write several possible transitions on each index card that help create a smooth flow.

Write Your First Draft

Write a first draft without worrying about mechanics or correctness. Write your sentences in logical order based on your index cards. Add appropriate transitions. Return to your pre-writing activities anytime you need to.

Edit and Revise Your Paragraph for Coherence

When you are finished, edit your paragraph for logical order and time or list transitions. Make a photocopy of your paragraph to bring to class.

Trade paragraphs with your partner. Edit each other's paragraph for logical order and appropriate transitions. Put your marks on the extra copy so that the writer can decide what changes to make to the original. As you read your partner's paragraph, ask yourself:

- Is the paragraph arranged by time or list order?
- Is it easy to follow the ideas?
- Is the order in which details are given logical? If not, how should the order be changed?
- Are there enough time or list transitions to create a smooth flow from one idea to the next?

Consider your partner's feedback. If you are unsure whether or how to edit your paragraph, consult with your instructor. Write your final copy of your paragraph to turn in to your instructor.

7

The New Medicines

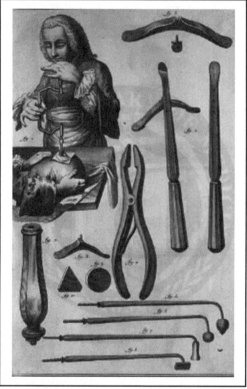

Courtesy of National Library of Medicine

Surgical instruments used in the late 1700s

"As to diseases make a habit of two things—to help, or at least, to do no harm."

—from *Epidemics* by Hippocrates, a Greek physician who lived 460–400 BCE. He is known as the father of modern scientific medicine.

Think about the Topic

- What did Hippocrates mean by "do no harm"?

- What are the most important medical issues in the world today?

- How will medicine and health care change in the next 50 years?

131

Reading 1: Medical Professionals Talk about Past and Future Medicine

In Your Writing Journal

Write this question at the top of a new page in your writing journal. Then write an answer based on your own knowledge and experience. Write as much as you can. Save your writing journal so you can add to it later.

How have medical advances changed people's lives?

Before You Read...

Discuss with Your Classmates

- What is the greatest medical accomplishment of the 20th century? How has it changed lives?
- What predictions can you make about medical accomplishments in the 21st century?
- What is the most serious medical problem that scientists should try to solve?
- Share your knowledge of current medical topics, such as cloning, stem cells, genetic manipulation, and testing.

Consider This Background Information

In the reading selection that follows, health-care professionals mention these terms:

- *Vaccination* (immunization): exposing the body to a small, safe amount of a disease, called a vaccine, so the body can build its own protection and be safe from the disease.
- *DNA:* the basic material in the cells of all living organisms. Its structure was discovered by James D. Watson and Francis Crick in 1953. DNA contains genetic information that makes each person different.
- *Genetic alteration:* changing the characteristics of a plant or animal by adding or removing a gene from its DNA.
- *Therapeutic abortion:* removal of an unborn baby from a woman's body because her health is in serious danger.

- *Stem cell technology:* the ability to use unspecialized cells from aborted embryos or healthy individuals to make specialized cells for parts of the body, such as heart muscle, brain tissue, and liver tissue.

- *Organ regeneration:* placing part of an organ from one person into another person's body, where it can grow to normal size.

- *Bioethics:* the study of moral questions and issues related to the fields of medicine and research.

Visit Your Writing Journal

What new ideas from your discussion can you add to your writing journal?

Step 1: Read for the Main Idea

First, read the selection quickly. Read it from beginning to end, and try to understand the writer's main idea and a few supporting ideas. Notice that some AWL words for vocabulary study are underlined. Underline any other words that are unfamiliar to you. Don't stop reading to look them up. Complete the outline at the end of the selection.

Medical Professionals Talk about Past and Future Medicine

marginalia

Since ancient times, new discoveries and advances in medicine have had the power to change lives and impact the world. Only a few hundred years ago, doctors believed that breathing bad air caused diseases. Today, technology and research are helping doctors and scientists find cures for diseases once considered incurable. Progress in the fields of medicine and biology has never occurred as rapidly as it does today.

This rapid progress brings new questions for medical professionals and all societies. Three medical professionals share their ideas about the past and future of medicine.

Renea Hushour is a nurse and emergency response expert. Her job is to make sure cities are ready for emergencies and disasters such as a bioterrorism attack. As a Red Cross

<u>volunteer</u>, she served in New York City after the 9/11 attack.

Dr. Oktay Cini, a heart surgeon, designs hospitals throughout the world. His goal is to make health-care facilities highly effective for patients and medical staff. He has designed hospitals in Moscow, Qatar, and throughout the Middle East.

Dr. Judith Westman is a researcher, pediatrician, and professor at the Ohio State University. She works with new medical students while she continues her genetic research. She specializes in cancer genetics.

Here's how these professionals responded to questions about past and future medicine.

Question: What is the greatest medical accomplishment of the 20th century, and how has it changed people's lives? What, if any, controversial issues did this accomplishment create?

Ms. Hushour: The greatest accomplishment is the development of vaccines to control infectious diseases such as diphtheria, pertussis, tetanus, yellow fever, influenza, polio, measles, smallpox, mumps, rubella, hepatitis A & B, roto-virus, and chicken pox. This saves thousands of lives each year worldwide, but many adults still die from diseases like influenza, pneumonia, hepatitis A, hepatitis B, and polio. These deaths are preventable with vaccines. Also, because vaccine-preventable diseases are at record lows, people have forgotten about the benefits of vaccinations.

Dr. Cini: The discovery of antibiotics is the most important event in medical history. Antibiotics have eliminated death due to many infectious diseases. Today, the overuse of antibiotics in some developing countries is a problem.

Dr. Westman: Watson and Crick's discovery of the structure of DNA has lead to the greatest changes. Genetic alterations in livestock and food products, the creation of designer drugs, improved therapies, prenatal diagnosis, and diagnosis of genetic disorders have impacted our lives. There are controversies over therapeutic abortion of <u>abnormal</u> pregnancies, cloning, and genetic <u>alterations</u> in livestock and food products.

Question: What predictions can you make about medical accomplishments in the 21ˢᵗ century? What new questions and issues will medical advances create? What controversial issues might arise?

Ms. Hushour: There will be Star Trek–ish advancements in stem cell technology and organ regeneration. We will need bioethics committees in hospitals and research facilities. There will be <u>controversies</u> over stem cell research, organ regeneration related to wealth, and the use of genetic knowledge to create superior people.

Dr. Cini: Stem cell and gene therapy will open a new era in the battle against many diseases. There will be many ethical issues. I fear the misuse of these new technologies if appropriate measures are not taken.

Dr. Westman: We will find out how our genes interact to cause the wide variety of humans that we have in our world. We already are challenged by issues of cloning, embryonic stem cells, and pregnancy <u>termination</u>.

Question: Regarding bioethics, Leon R. Kass, Chair of the President's Council on Bioethics, writes, "So long as no one is hurt, no one's will is <u>violated</u>, and no one is excluded or discriminated against, there may be little to worry about." What are your thoughts on his statement?

Ms. Hushour: Bioethics, in my opinion, is inseparable from embracing tolerance and diversity. For all our country's strengths, we continue to struggle desperately with tolerance and diversity.

Dr. Cini: The simplicity of the statement scares me. It accepts that there might be little to worry about. I would like to know what "little" is or will be.

Dr. Westman: Mr. Kass presents a very western approach to bioethics with an <u>emphasis</u> on individual rights. Less-developed countries must also consider the effect on society and economics. How much is one life worth? Should one life be saved for the price that could provide immunizations to 500 children?

Sources: Oktay Cini, Questionnaire and Interview, September 2004.
    Renea Hushour, Questionnaire and Interview, December 2004.
    Judith A. Westman, Questionnaire and Interview, August 2004.

Although this is an interview, you can still identify the topic and main idea. You may want to reread paragraphs one and two. Complete this outline:

The topic: _____

                                  Write a word or phrase.

The main idea: _____

                                  Write a sentence about the main idea.

                                  _____

Some supporting ideas: _____

                                  Write a different phrase or sentence on each line.

                                  _____

                                  _____

Do the supporting ideas help prove the main idea?

Step 2: Read for New Words

Return to Appendix A to review vocabulary-building strategies.

AWL Words to Know

These AWL words in order of their appearance are underlined in the reading selection. Add them to your vocabulary journal.

impact	alterations	violated
volunteer	controversies	emphasis
abnormal	termination	

Next, add any unfamiliar words that you underlined in Reading 1.

Follow these steps to complete your vocabulary journal:

1. Write the word and the sentence in the reading containing the word.
2. Note what part of speech the word should be based on its place in the sentence.
3. Guess the meaning of the word based on the sentence's meaning and the main idea of the reading selection.
4. Discuss your guess with your instructor and classmates, and confirm your guess by looking up the word in the dictionary. Add any notes that will help you remember the meaning of the word.
5. Use the word in your own original sentence.
6. Gloss the reading selection before reading it a second time.

Step 3: Read for Answers

Reread Reading 1, and add marginalia in the wide right-hand margin. Then return to the reading to find the information that you need to complete this exercise. Prepare to discuss your answers.

Organize the responses from each person by completing the chart.

	Ms. Hushour	**Dr. Cini**	**Dr. Westman**
Job			*pediatrician, genetic researcher, professor*
Greatest medical accomplishment in 20th century			
Prediction for 21st century	*bioethics committees in hospitals and research facilities*	*ethical issues*	
Issues or controversies in the 21st century		*misuse of new technology*	
Reaction to Mr. Kass's statement about bioethics			*cost of one life in western countries vs. cost of immunizations for 500 children*

Step 4: Read between the Lines

Which respondent do you think would make these statements? Remember to think about the <u>respondent's opinion</u>, not your own opinion. Circle your answer. Some questions may have more than one answer. Prepare to give reasons for your answers.

1. Adults should receive influenza vaccine.

   Ms. Hushour   Dr. Cini   Dr. Westman

2. The discovery of DNA has caused some controversies, but it has also helped researchers learn more.

   Ms. Hushour   Dr. Cini   Dr. Westman

3. Medical advances will create new ethical questions and controversies.
   Ms. Hushour   Dr. Cini   Dr. Westman

4. New health-care facilities should be safe from bioterrorism.
   Ms. Hushour   Dr. Cini   Dr. Westman

5. The needs of patients and doctors should be considered before a new hospital is built.
   Ms. Hushour   Dr. Cini   Dr. Westman

6. Wealthier people will be more likely to receive regeneration services.
   Ms. Hushour   Dr. Cini   Dr. Westman

Step 5: Respond to the Reading

Reflect on your own knowledge and experience, and answer the questions. Remember to think about <u>your own opinions</u>. Be ready to discuss your answers.

1. Which of the three respondents would you most like to interview? What questions would you ask?

2. Dr. Westman suggests that people should think about the cost of medicine and how people might benefit. Read the situation and write your decision.

   You have enough money to save one life or to provide vaccine against a deadly disease for 500 children in a less-developed country. How would you use your money? What factors would you consider to make this decision? What if the life you could save were the life of an elderly family member?

Return to Your Writing Journal

Return to your writing journal, and review your response to the opening question for Reading 1. What new ideas and opinions do you have now? How is your life different from your parents' lives as a result of medical advances? What are some positive effects of medical advances made during your lifetime? What are some negative effects of medical advances made during your lifetime? Add your new thoughts to your response. Write as much as you can.

Reading 2: Fast Forward to 2020: What to Expect in Molecular Medicine

In Your Writing Journal

Write this question at the top of a new page in your writing journal. Then write an answer based on your own knowledge and experience. Write as much as you can. Save your writing journal so you can add to it later.

How will medical advances in the near future affect the lives of ordinary people?

Before You Read...

Discuss with Your Classmates

- How is a person's appearance determined?
- Why is genetic research important? How might it be misused?
- Is it possible to free the world of disease?

Consider This Background Information

- Genes determine a person's appearance—height, hair color, skin color, and eye color. Mental abilities, natural talents, and susceptibility to certain diseases are also affected by genes.
- DNA is the basic material in the cells of all living organisms. A person's DNA includes his or her genetic information.
- The Human Genome Project (HGP) was completed in 2003. It identifies the genes and their sequence in humans.
- Bioethics, sometimes called medical ethics, is the study of moral issues in the fields of medical treatment and research. The idea of medical ethics was first suggested by Hippocrates, a Greek physician who lived from 460 to 400 BCE.
- The Ethical, Legal and Social Implications (ELSI) Research Program addresses issues related to the Human Genome Project.

Visit Your Writing Journal

What new ideas from your discussion can you add to your writing journal?

Step 1: Read for the Main Idea

First, read the selection quickly. Read it from beginning to end, and try to understand the writer's main idea and a few supporting ideas. Notice that some AWL words for vocabulary study are underlined. Underline any other words that are unfamiliar to you. Don't stop reading to look them up. Complete the outline at the end of the selection.

Fast Forward to 2020: What to Expect in Molecular Medicine

marginalia

In 2003, molecular biologists completed the human genome project (HGP). The HGP identified all 30,000 genes in DNA and their sequence. The human genome, which is all of the genetic material in a human cell, is available on the Internet to anyone interested. A few years after completion, this knowledge has already begun to <u>revolutionize</u> biology and medicine.

The U.S. government's Department of Energy has made predictions in four <u>areas</u> about what we might expect by 2020. These areas are: drugs, medical knowledge, genetic testing and therapy, and <u>fundamental</u> biology.

First, there will be more effective drugs. In 2000, there were about 500 drugs; by 2020 there will be at least six times as many drugs based on DNA technology. Instead of using drugs to treat diseases after they are <u>contracted</u>, doctors will use drugs to prevent or delay diseases. Doctors will know which diseases a person is likely to contract because a person's medical record will include his or her complete genetic profile. This genetic profile will also tell doctors which drugs will work effectively for an individual. Furthermore, individualized drugs will reduce deaths and eliminate most side effects related to drugs.

The second prediction concerns the impact knowledge of individuals' DNA might have on society. This knowledge may be available to others outside the medical profession, such as employers and insurance companies. Employers may refuse to hire someone who is likely to become seriously ill. Insurance companies may <u>deny</u> insurance to applicants who have high risk for certain diseases. The effect on a person's life will be <u>dramatic</u>.

Third, genetic testing and gene therapy will become common. Abnormal genes that cause certain diseases will be replaced with normal genes. It will be possible to grow cells and some organs for transplantation. Genetic testing will be routine for mistaken identity, paternity, and criminal identification. Certain behaviors will be explained by a person's genes. Courts will have difficult decisions to make about criminal behavior as a consequence of free will or genetic <u>constitution</u>. The use of genetic information will become part of everyday life.

Finally, the most important consequence of the genome project will be a much greater understanding of fundamental biology. By 2020, perhaps 1000 genomes will be completed. This knowledge will <u>enable</u> scientists to cure diseases such as Parkinson's and Alzheimer's. In addition, the potential will exist for solving other problems including environmental cleanup.

The progress made by 2020 will improve human health, yet it will also bring <u>challenges</u> and the possibility of misuse. Society as a whole, not just the genome scientists, will be faced with new challenges never imagined a short time ago.

Source: from Daniel Drell and Anne Adamson, "Fast Forward to 2020: What to Expect in Molecular Medicine," Human Genome Project Information, December 2004. *www.ornl.gov/sci/techresources/Human_Genome/medicine/tnty.shtml*

Based on your first reading, complete this outline:

The topic:
_____
Write a word or phrase.

The main idea:
_____
Write a sentence about the main idea.

_____

Some supporting ideas:
_____
Write a different phrase or sentence on each line.

_____

_____

Do the supporting ideas help prove the main idea?

Step 2: Read for New Words

Return to Appendix A to review vocabulary-building strategies.

AWL Words to Know

These AWL words in order of appearance are underlined in the reading selection. Add them to your vocabulary journal.

revolutionize	contracted	constitution
areas	deny	enable
fundamental	dramatic	challenges

Next, add any unfamiliar words that you underlined in Reading 2.

Follow these steps to complete your vocabulary journal:

1. Write the word and the sentence in the reading containing the word.
2. Note what part of speech the word should be based on its place in the sentence.
3. Guess the meaning of the word based on the sentence's meaning and the main idea of the reading selection.
4. Discuss your guess with your instructor and classmates, and confirm your guess by looking up the word in the dictionary. Add any notes that will help you remember the meaning of the word.
5. Use the word in your own original sentence.
6. Gloss the reading selection before reading it a second time.

Step 3: Read for Answers

Reread Reading 1, and add marginalia in the wide right-hand margin. Then return to the reading to find the information that you need to complete this exercise. Prepare to discuss your answers.

1. Complete the chart by adding an example of a medical practice expected by 2020 in each of the areas identified by the Department of Energy.

Medical Topic	Example
Drugs	
Medical knowledge	
Genetic testing and therapy	
Fundamental biology	*solve problems of environmental cleanup*

2. How can knowledge of an individual's genetic information affect his or her life positively?

3. How can knowledge of an individual's genetic information affect his or her life negatively?

4. A greater understanding of fundamental biology is considered the most important consequence of the Human Genome Project. Why?

Step 4: Read between the Lines

Do you think the writer of Reading 2 would agree or disagree with these statements? Return to the reading to discover the writer's opinion, and then circle A for agree or D for disagree. Prepare to give reasons for your answers. Remember to think about the underline{writer's opinion}, not your own opinion.

1. Eventually, the completion of the Human Genome Project will have more impact on our lives than other medical accomplishments.   A   D

2. It is difficult to make predictions about changes resulting from the completion of the Human Genome Project.   A   D

3. The care that doctors offer patients will not change as a result of the completion of the Human Genome Project.   A   D

4. Some results of the completion of the Human Genome Project may be problematic.   A   D

5. Scientists will have the greatest responsibility for solving problems created by the completion of the Human Genome Project.   A   D

Step 5: Respond to the Reading

Reflect on your own knowledge and experience, and answer the questions. Remember to think about your own opinions. Be ready to discuss your answers.

1. How will the completion of the Human Genome Project affect you and members of your family?

2. What other medical accomplishments have improved people's lives but also created controversies?

Return to Your Writing Journal

Return to your writing journal, and review your responses to each of the questions for Reading 2. What new ideas and opinions do you have now? In what ways will the effects of future medical advances be positive? What is most troubling about future medical advances? How will your own life be different as a result of future medical advances? Add your new thoughts to your response. Write as much as you can.

Writing Workshop: Concluding the Paragraph

By now, you have learned about the important elements of a paragraph. As a writer, you know that it is your job to help the reader understand what you are saying. A topic sentence will tell the reader your topic and your attitude about it. Support sentences will give details to help the reader understand your ideas about your topic. After you have given the reader enough information for a clear understanding, it is time to end the paragraph. It is important that the reader not be left hanging. The writer's last task is to tell the reader that the paragraph is complete by writing a concluding sentence, the last sentence of the paragraph.

The Concluding Sentence

A paragraph should not stop suddenly; the writer must tell the reader the paragraph is complete. A writer uses a concluding sentence to signal the end of the paragraph. In the concluding sentence, a writer frequently restates the idea expressed in the topic sentence using different words. Restating the topic sentence reminds the reader of what the paragraph was about. Just like the topic sentence, it should state the topic and the controlling idea. The concluding sentence should never introduce a new idea or detail.

Now look at paragraph four in Reading 2 on pages 141–42. The idea in the topic sentence and the concluding sentence are very similar. Both the topic and concluding sentences tell the reader that genetic knowledge will change people's lives.

Compare the topic sentence and the concluding sentence in paragraph five on page 142.

Topic sentence: Third, genetic testing and gene therapy will become common.

Concluding sentence: The use of genetic information will become part of everyday life.

What is the main idea of both of these sentences?

Writing Activity 1: Practice Identifying Concluding Sentences

Read each topic sentence, and decide if the second sentence is an appropriate concluding sentence.

1. The completion of the human genome is the greatest achievement of modern medicine.
   Understanding the human genome will change medicine more than any other medical discovery.

   yes   no

2. Millions of adults in the United States cannot read well enough to fill out a job application form.
   Homeless children often do not have the opportunity for formal education.

   yes   no

3. Daily exercise is important if a person wants to participate in a sport.
   A regular exercise program can help make a person successful in a sport.

   yes   no

4. Going to college requires a lot of time for studying.
   Going to college also requires plenty of money.

   yes   no

5. Babies require almost constant attention.
   A new mother will discover that she has little time for herself because babies are very demanding.

   yes   no

Writing Activity 2: Practice Writing Concluding Sentences

Look at each topic sentence, and write an appropriate concluding sentence.

1. The increase in college tuition will be a hardship for many students.

2. Although vaccines are available for many diseases, many poorer countries cannot afford them.

3. Cats make better pets than dogs because they are easier to take care of.

4. Teenage drivers should not be permitted to drive after midnight.

   <u>Remember</u>: As a writer, you must help the reader understand exactly what you are saying in your paragraph. Tell the reader when the paragraph is complete. This is done with a concluding sentence that reminds the reader of the topic and controlling idea. The concluding sentence should never introduce a new idea or detail.

Time to Write

In this paragraph, you will use everything you have learned about writing a unified, coherent paragraph with concrete and specific support. Finally, you will end your paragraph with an appropriate concluding sentence that lets the reader know that the paragraph is complete.

Start Your Paragraph

Now return to your writing journal. Read over your responses to the opening journal questions for Readings 1 and 2. Choose one response to develop in a paragraph. Identify the topic of your paragraph, add a controlling idea, and write your topic sentence.

Return to your writing journal to gather details that support your topic sentence. Make a list of the details you will include. Check the details you have selected for unity. Should any be eliminated because they are off-topic? Consider the order in which you will arrange your details. Will you use list or time order? Number your details to show the order in which they will appear in your paragraph. Make a note of where transitions are needed. What transitions will you use? Look back at the transitions listed in Chapters 5 and 6 for ideas.

Write Your First Draft

After you have checked your details for unity and selected an organization order, write a first draft without worrying about mechanics or correctness. Write your sentences in logical order and add appropriate transitions to help the reader move through your paragraph smoothly. Add a concluding sentence that reminds the reader of the topic and the controlling idea.

Edit and Revise Your Paragraph

When you have finished, edit your paragraph for unity, coherence, and support. Next, examine your concluding sentence. Does it remind the reader of your topic and controlling idea? In other words, does it state the topic sentence in different words? Make a photocopy of your paragraph to bring to class.

Trade paragraphs with your partner. First, edit the concluding sentence of each other's paragraph. Read only the topic sentence and concluding sentence. After reading your partner's topic and concluding sentences, ask yourself:

Does the topic sentence identify the topic and controlling idea?

Does the concluding sentence remind the reader of the same topic and controlling idea?

Has the writer kept new ideas and details out of the concluding sentence?

Now read your partner's entire paragraph and edit it for unity, coherence, and support as you have in previous chapters. Put your marks on the extra copy so that the writer can decide what changes to make to the original.

Consider your partner's feedback. If you are unsure whether or how to edit your paragraph, consult with your instructor. Write your final copy of your paragraph to turn in to your instructor.

8

Artists' Perspectives of Spring

Courtesy of Joshua Hall, age 7, Crestwood, KY

One Child's Perspective

"In the spring a young man's fancy lightly turns to thoughts of love."

—Alfred Lord Tennyson,
"Locksley Hall" (1842)

A Romantic's Perspective

Think about the Topic

- What might influence a person's perspective of spring?
- What is your perspective of spring?
- What is special about an artist's perspective?

Reading 1: A Novelist's Perspective of Spring

In Your Writing Journal

In this chapter, the reading selections offer two different perspectives of spring. The writer of each selection has his or her own way of thinking about spring; likewise, you have your own ideas about spring. First, write your own description of spring. Then, **after** *completing each reading selection, you will add to your description.*

Write this question at the top of a new page in your writing journal. Then write an answer based on your own knowledge and experience. Write as much as you can. Save your writing journal so you can add to it later.

> *Describe spring in either your native country or your second country.*

Before You Read...

Discuss with Your Classmates

- What have you gained from reading fiction?
- What is your favorite story, and why do you like it?
- If you were asked to write about one season of the year, which would you choose? Why? How would you describe the arrival of that season?
- Make a guess about what the phrase "a false spring" means.

Consider This Background Information

- Ernest Hemingway, an American novelist, lived from 1899 to 1961.
- In 1954, he won the Nobel Prize for Literature.
- He is well known for his many stories and novels.
- His simple and direct writing style is probably the most imitated of any American writer in the 20th century.
- *A Moveable Feast* was written in the late 1950s and published in 1964 after Hemingway's death. It is based on his experiences while living in Paris, France, in the 1920s. This reading selection is taken from a chapter entitled "A False Spring."

Step 1: Read for the Main Idea

First, read the selection quickly. Read it from beginning to end, and try to understand the writer's main idea and a few supporting ideas. There are no AWL words, but you may find some unfamiliar words. Underline and study them before doing your careful reading. Complete the outline at the end of the selection.

"A False Spring" from *A Moveable Feast*

Ernest Hemingway

marginalia

With so many trees in the city, you could see the spring coming each day until a night of warm wind would bring it suddenly in one morning. Sometimes the heavy cold rains would beat it back so that it would seem that it would never come and that you were losing a season out of your life. This was the only truly sad time in Paris because it was unnatural. You expected to be sad in the fall. Part of you died each year when the leaves fell from the trees and their branches were bare against the wind and the cold, wintry light. But you knew there would always be the spring, as you knew the river would flow again after it was frozen. When the cold rains kept on and killed the spring, it was as though a young person had died for no reason.

In those days, though, the spring always came finally but it was frightening that it had nearly failed.

Based on your first reading, complete this outline:

The topic: _____

Write a word or phrase.

The main idea: _____

Write a complete sentence that tells the main idea.

_____

Some supporting ideas: _____

Write a different phrase or sentence on each line.

_____

_____

Do the supporting ideas help prove the main idea?

Step 2: Read for New Words

Return to Appendix A to review vocabulary-building strategies.

This reading selection has no AWL words. What words did you underline as unfamiliar? Add your underlined words to your vocabulary journal.

Follow these steps to complete your vocabulary journal:

1. Write the word and the sentence in the reading containing the word.
2. Note what part of speech the word should be based on its place in the sentence.
3. Guess the meaning of the word based on the sentence's meaning and the main idea of the reading selection.
4. Discuss your guess with your instructor and classmates, and confirm your guess by looking up the word in the dictionary. Add any notes that will help you remember the meaning of the word.
5. Use the word in your own original sentence.
6. Gloss the reading selection before reading it a second time.

Step 3: Read for Answers

Reread Reading 1, and add marginalia in the wide right-hand margin. Then return to the reading to find the information that you need to complete this exercise. Prepare to discuss your answers.

1. How could you see the spring coming?

2. Why would it later seem that it wouldn't come?

3. Why was it natural to be sad in the fall?

4. Why was it unnatural to be sad in the spring?

Step 4: Read between the Lines

Do you think the writer of Reading 1 would agree or disagree with these statements? Return to the reading to discover the writer's opinion, and then circle A for agree or D for disagree. Prepare to give reasons for your answers. Remember to think about the <u>writer's opinion</u>, not your own opinion.

1. Changes in the trees indicate a change in seasons.	A	D
2. Life in Paris was often sad.	A	D
3. Winter is a joyful season.	A	D
4. The death of a young person is more sorrowful than the death of an old person.	A	D
5. Without spring to follow winter, life would be depressing.	A	D
6. People expect nature to always follow the same pattern.	A	D

Step 5: Respond to the Reading

Reflect on your own knowledge and experience, and answer the questions. Remember to think about <u>your own opinions</u>. Be ready to discuss your answers.

1. According to Hemingway, fall brings sadness; the delay of spring brings sadness and also fear. Do you agree or disagree with Hemingway's statement? Why?

2. How are a false spring and the death of a young person similar?

3. What does Hemingway mean by, "Part of you died each year when the leaves fell from the trees. . . ."?

Return to Your Writing Journal

Return to your writing journal, and review your response to the opening question for Reading 1. What new ideas and opinions do you have now? Hemingway's view of spring reflects his feelings. What are your feelings about spring? Add your new thoughts to your response. Write as much as you can.

Reading 2: A Poet's Perspective of Spring

In Your Writing Journal

Do not add to your writing journal before reading the selection. After you have completed this reading selection, add your new ideas to the description of spring you wrote at the beginning of this chapter.

Before You Read...

Discuss with Your Classmates

- How does poetry differ from prose?
- What might the goal of a poet be?
- Have you read a poem that affected you? How did it affect you?
- Think about the title of this poem, "Nothing Gold Can Stay." What does it mean to you?
- What perspective of spring do you expect from a poet?

Consider This Background Information

- Robert Frost, an American poet, lived from 1874 to 1963.
- Throughout most of his life, he was a farmer and teacher.
- As a farmer, he developed an avid interest in botany (the study of plants).
- At the age of 40, his poems were still unknown in the United States, so he moved to England.
- In England his work was recognized and soon after became famous in the United States.
- He received four Pulitzer Prizes for poetry collections published in 1924, 1930, 1936, and 1942.
- The 1924 Pulitzer was awarded to *New Hampshire,* published in 1923, which included the poem, "Nothing Gold Can Stay."

Step 1: Read for the Main Ideas

Listen as your teacher reads the poem aloud. Read this poem aloud to yourself a few times. Try to grasp its main idea. With a classmate, take turns reading the poem aloud. Listen to its rhyme and rhythm.

NOTHING GOLD CAN STAY

Robert Frost

marginalia

Nature's first green is gold,
Her hardest hue to hold.
Her early leaf's a flower;
But only so an hour.
Then leaf subsides to leaf.
So Eden sank to grief,
So dawn goes down to day.
Nothing gold can stay.

Poems, like prose, have main ideas and supporting ideas. Based on your first reading, complete the outline:

The topic: _____

                                    Write a word or phrase.

The main idea: _____

                                    Write a complete sentence that tells the main idea.

                                    _____

Some supporting ideas: _____

                                    Write a different phrase or sentence on each line.

                                    _____

Do the supporting ideas help prove the main idea?

Step 2: Read for New Words

Return to Appendix A to review vocabulary-building strategies.

This reading selection has no AWL words. For this selection, Step 2 and Step 3 should be done together. In Step 2 you will use your dictionary to discover Frost's meaning. Step 3 is similar to the glossing you have been doing in earlier chapters.

Step 3: Read for Answers

For your careful reading of this selection, use the copy of the poem that follows. Working with a partner will be helpful. Prepare to discuss your answers.

1. Working with your dictionary, take the poem apart. Translate words. Work for deeper understanding. Write an explanation of each line below it. If you have no idea what a line means, leave it blank and move on. You can explore the lines you do not understand during class discussion. The first line is already explained.

Nature's first green is gold,
On trees and shrubs the buds are gold before they turn green.

Her hardest hue to hold.

Her early leaf's a flower;

But only so an hour.

Then leaf subsides to leaf.

So Eden sank to grief,

So dawn goes down to day.

Nothing gold can stay.

2. Now return to the whole poem, and read it aloud to yourself again. How would you summarize its main idea?

Step 4: Read between the Lines

Making inferences involves figuring out a writer's unstated meaning. After reading, listening to, and discussing "Nothing Gold Can Stay," work with a partner to answer the questions. Prepare to give reasons for your answers.

1. Tone is the feeling a writer creates with his or her choice of words. Sad, happy, angry, and funny are a few examples of different tones a writer might create. In your opinion, what is the tone of the poem?

2. In the sixth line, Frost mentions Eden, or the Garden of Eden, the original home of the first man and the first woman, according to the Bible. Why do you think Frost includes a religious reference in a poem about nature?

3. Write one sentence that expresses Frost's perspective of spring.

Step 5: Respond to the Reading

Reflect on your own knowledge and experience, and answer the questions. Remember to think about your own opinions. Be ready to discuss your answers.

1. *Nature* refers to the world of living things and the outdoors. Nature is generally treated as a female. Frost does this in his second line: "**Her** hardest hue to hold." Why do you think nature is considered female rather than male?

2. What is true about Frost's poem? What seems strange or confusing?

3. With a partner, describe any poem with which you are familiar and explain how you feel when you read it.

Return to Your Writing Journal

Return to your writing journal, and review your response to the opening question. What new ideas and opinions do you have now? Frost uses comparisons to describe spring. To what can you compare spring? What can you add to your description of spring? Write as much as you can.

Writing Workshop: Writing a Descriptive Paragraph

You have learned the important elements of writing an academic paragraph. For this writing assignment you will write a descriptive paragraph. First, review the characteristics of a well-written paragraph.

- A paragraph has a topic sentence with a controlling idea. It tells the reader the topic and the writer's attitude about the topic.
- It is thoroughly developed with concrete and specific details.
- It is unified. There are no sentences that are off-topic.
- It is coherent. Sentences are arranged in a logical order, and the paragraph has a smooth flow created by using transitions.
- A paragraph ends with a concluding sentence.

The Descriptive Paragraph

The descriptive paragraph has a special purpose: to give the reader a clear and vivid mental picture of a person, place, thing, or idea. A clear mental picture appeals to the senses. Instead of simply telling, the writer "shows" how something looks, sounds, smells, feels, and tastes by giving plenty of concrete and specific description. A writer must choose adjectives, adverbs, and verbs that describe accurately. Words like *good, bad, beautiful, ugly, nice,* and *interesting* are too vague to give the reader a clear picture. As a writer, you can improve your descriptions by asking yourself questions about your topic. Consider these vague sentences, followed by more descriptive sentences. Notice that there are questions a writer can answer in order to make description more vivid.

The room smelled bad.
Questions: How bad did the room smell? What did it smell like?
The room smelled like a garbage can stuffed with rotten eggs.

Everyone liked her beautiful wedding dress.
Questions: In what way was the dress beautiful? How much did everyone like it?
No one could take their eyes off of her sparkling, pure white wedding dress.

The music was very loud.
Questions: How loud was the music? What kind of music was it?
The ear-splitting rock music was loud enough to hear throughout the neighborhood.

The boss spoke unpleasantly and gave too many orders to his employee.
Questions: What did he sound like? How many orders did he give? What kind of boss was he?
Every few minutes, the demanding boss growled enough orders for ten employees to one frightened employee.

Now, return to Reading 1 and notice how Hemingway describes the arrival of spring and his feelings when it seems that spring will not arrive.

To Describe	Hemingway Uses
a lot of rain	heavy cold rains
the rain stopped spring	heavy cold rains beat it back
he was sad that it wasn't spring yet	it would seem that you were losing a season of your life
cold rain prevented spring	it was as though a young person had died for no reason

In Reading 2, Frost also describes spring but with fewer words than used in prose.

To Describe	Frost Uses
the first buds of spring	Nature's first green is gold
the first buds and leaves do not last very long	But only so an hour. Nothing gold can stay.

Writing Activity 1: Practice Using Sensory Description

Rewrite these nondescriptive sentences using descriptive words to create a clear mental picture for the reader. Ask yourself questions to help write better descriptions.

1. The storm made a lot of noise.

   The storm startled us with crashes of thunder every few minutes.

2. The snowfall was beautiful.

3. The sofa was uncomfortable.

4. My sister's bedroom is messy.

5. Winter is an unpleasant season.

A Dominant Impression

A descriptive paragraph should leave the reader with a dominant impression. This means a writer focuses on creating a single picture of the topic. This is the impression the reader will remember after reading the paragraph because the writer has used enough concrete and specific details to create a clear mental picture. The reader should understand whether the writer's attitude is negative or positive. For example, if you are describing rain, the reader needs to know if you think the rain is frightening or calming. A reader will not have a clear picture of a meal if you describe it as both delicious and sickening. The dominant impression should be clear in the topic sentence. After the writer states the dominant impression in the topic sentence, he or she illustrates it with carefully selected details in the support sentences.

Again, think about Reading 1 from *A Moveable Feast*. Which sentence best expresses Hemingway's dominant impression of spring?

   a. Spring is a time of joy and newness.
   b. It is sad when it seems that spring is not coming.
   c. Fall is a bad season.

Look at Reading 2, "Nothing Gold Can Stay." Which sentence best expresses Frost's dominant impression of spring?

   a. Spring's beauty does not last long.
   b. Spring is the best time of the year.
   c. Everything looks like gold in spring.

Writing Activity 2: Practice Creating a Dominant Impression

1. To create the dominant impression that winter is a joyless and unbearable season, which words and phrases should be included? Circle them.

grey clouds every day

animals sleep through winter

birds sing and dig for worms

dirty piles of snow

dangerous ice-covered streets

warm, delicious hot chocolate

days are short and nights are long

gorgeous ice-covered trees glisten

coldness keeps everyone inside

2. Read the paragraph and think about the dominant impression.

The first signs of spring are easy to miss. In fact, only a careful observer of spring is going to see them. Who else would notice that the tiny buds on many shrubs and trees have changed from their winter grey to radiant gold? And only spring's most diligent student will catch sight of the first red-breasted robins hurriedly mining for worms in the pale lawn. Without walking outdoors, one can tell that the days seem a little bit longer or the afternoons are a bit warmer, but these aren't reliable signs of spring. They are often just a tease to the winter-weary. It takes a walk in the woods to catch the greening of the undergrowth, the small umbrella-like may apples sending up their bright shoots and the new young ferns unfolding their tendrils near the creek. These are the signs that can be trusted. The true lover of spring knows the delicate perfume of her tender arrival, doesn't miss the first moments of certainty, and knows when to rejoice.

Write a sentence expressing the dominant impression.

<u>Remember</u>: As a writer, you must help the reader "see" a clear mental picture of what you are describing. Create a dominant impression that the reader will remember. Use plenty of descriptive concrete and specific details to create a memorable mental picture.

Time to Write

In this paragraph you will write your own description of spring. Your paragraph should give the reader a dominate impression and include plenty of sensory description.

Start Your Paragraph

Now return to your writing journal. Read your description of spring. After reading your description, you probably have some idea about the dominant impression you want to create for the reader. Write a topic sentence that clearly identifies the dominant impression. The dominant impression serves as the controlling idea.

Return to your writing journal to gather details that support your topic sentence. Make a list of details to include. Examine your list and experiment with different words and phrases that describe. Try to use descriptive words that will appeal to the five senses. Ask yourself questions similar to the ones on pages 160–61.

Write Your First Draft

Write a first draft without worrying about mechanics or correctness. Focus on creating a clear mental picture for the reader. What is the dominant impression the reader will remember after reading your paragraph? Return to your list of descriptive details anytime you need to.

Edit and Revise Your Paragraph

When you have finished, edit your paragraph for descriptive support. Make a photocopy of your paragraph to bring to class.

Trade paragraphs with your partner. Guess your partner's dominant impression. Is it the dominant impression he or she intended?

Now read your partner's entire paragraph, and underline the nouns. Put your marks on the extra copy so that the writer can decide what changes to make to the original. Consider each noun and ask yourself:

Is the noun described adequately?

Do I have a clear mental picture of this noun?

What else could the writer say about this noun?

Does this description contribute to the dominant impression?

After considering the description, edit the paragraph for unity and coherence.

Consider your partner's feedback. If you are unsure whether or how to edit your paragraph, consult with your instructor. Write your final copy of your paragraph to turn in to your instructor.

Appendix A: Vocabulary-Building Strategies and Sample Student Journal Entries

Vocabulary-Building Strategies

Reading and writing assignments offer college students valuable opportunities to increase their knowledge in a particular subject area and demonstrate their ability to organize, retain, and respond to the information they have learned. To language students, reading and writing assignments also offer necessary opportunities to advance their mastery of the language and increase the skill with which they manage the written word. Both kinds of learning—acquisition of knowledge and language mastery—require patience, persistence, and one other very important raw material: vocabulary!

After each reading of the text, in Step 2: Read for New Words, AWL (Academic Word List) vocabulary have been pre-selected for your study. You have also been invited to select additional words that are unfamiliar to you. For these words to be added to your active vocabulary, they first must be added to your vocabulary journal.

In Step 2, you will find a series of steps to take as you add each word to your vocabulary journal. In order to complete these steps successfully, it is important for you to understand two vocabulary-building strategies: using context clues and using the dictionary.

Context Clues

Using the Meaning of the Surrounding Text

When you need to read quickly to gather main ideas, it isn't wise to stop to look up unfamiliar words in your dictionary. Not only is it possible, but it is also advisable for you to guess the meaning of many of the unfamiliar words based on their place in the sentence and the surrounding words and sentences. When you do this, you are using context clues. **Context clues**

167

are the other words and sentences surrounding an unfamiliar word. The context in which a word is found is sometimes loaded with information that can help you discover the meaning of an unfamiliar word. When you come to an unfamiliar word while you are reading, ask yourself:

- What word makes sense in the sentence?

- Does my guess fit with the general meaning of the reading selection?

Practice This Strategy

First, guess the meaning of the italicized word in the sentence. You do not have to be able to say the word to understand the meaning. Ask yourself the preceding questions. Make several guesses for the italicized word in each sentence. Notice that more clues are given in Sentences 1b and 2b. How will this improve your guess?

    1. a. The children were *fretful*.

        Guesses: _____

      b. The children were *fretful* because they couldn't find their favorite toys.

        Guesses: _____

    2. a. Doctors should *scrutinize* a new medicine.

        Guesses: _____

      b. Doctors should *scrutinize* a new medicine so they will understand any problems the medicine can cause.

        Guesses: _____

Discuss your guesses with your classmates and your teacher. Which guesses do you think are more accurate—guesses for the a sentences or the b sentences? Why?

Using Parts of Speech

Here is another question that will make your guesses more accurate:

- What kind of word should the unfamiliar word be? Should it be a noun, verb, adjective, or adverb?

The different kinds of words in a language are called **parts of speech.** The parts of speech perform different jobs in a sentence. In your grammar study, you have learned about nouns, verbs, adjectives, adverbs, and prepositions—all parts of speech. You also know some things about English sentence structure. You can use this knowledge when you guess the meanings of unfamiliar words.

Think about how the parts of speech are used in sentences. Pay careful attention to the location of the unfamiliar word in the sentence. Study the sentences and explanations. Answer the questions:

1. *unfamiliar word* should talk with a guidance counselor or financial advisor before paying fees to scholarship companies.

   When an unfamiliar word is at the beginning of a statement sentence, it is usually the subject of the sentence. What parts of speech can be used for subjects?

   _____

2. Others provide nothing for the student's advance fee—not even a list of *unfamiliar word* sources; still others tell students they've been selected as "finalists" for awards that require an up-front fee.

   When an unfamiliar word comes before a noun, it usually describes the noun. What part of speech is used to describe a noun?

   _____

3. Some company representatives are *unfamiliar word* to answer a student's questions.

   When an unfamiliar word comes after a subject and the *be* verb, it usually describes the subject of the sentence. What part of speech is used to describe subjects in this sentence pattern?

   _____

4. The Federal Trade Commission *unfamiliar word* students about giving out checking account or credit card information.

   When an unfamiliar word comes after the subject of the sentence, it usually describes an action or a state of being. What part of speech is used to describe an action or a state of being?

   _____

Practice This Strategy

The text that follows uses some nonsense words in italics. Read the text and answer the questions. Remember to think about the meaning of the sentence, the general meaning of the reading selection, and the kind of word needed based on the sentence structure.

> In the spring of 1974, Della Adams was *shraaft* while she was on a long trip aboard a cruise ship. As soon as she *carrumped* home from her trip, she visited her doctor. After examining her, he *plited* her condition as simple motion sickness. Of course, his *plitation* caused her great relief, and very soon she was feeling perfectly *steap* again.

If these nonsense words were real words, what part of speech would they be? If these nonsense words had real meanings, what could they be?

	Part of Speech	Possible Meaning
1. shraaft	_____	_____
2. carrump	_____	_____
3. plite	_____	_____
4. plitation	_____	_____
5. steap	_____	_____

Discuss your answers with your classmates. Did you give similar answers?

Using the Dictionary

Which Dictionary?

An ESL dictionary is a good choice for language learners. The definitions in an ESL dictionary are easier to understand than those in regular English dictionaries. Grammar information and sample sentences are also provided. ESL dictionary writers are familiar with the vocabulary needs of language students. Your instructor can recommend an ESL dictionary.

It is common for language students to also use a translation dictionary. Sometimes there is no one-word translation for a particular word. When you use a translation dictionary, remember to look for meaning rather than a single word for the unfamiliar English word. It's always a good idea to discuss meanings with your classmates and instructor.

Choosing the Correct Meaning

Most English words have more than one meaning. When this is the case, you need to decide which definition (meaning) fits the unfamiliar word you are studying. To do this, you need to use the context in which the unfamiliar word is found. First, decide the part of speech of the word by looking at the sentence containing the word. Then look at the definitions given in your dictionary. Check each definition with the sentence. Pay careful attention to the example sentences in the dictionary entry. Sometimes these examples may help more than the definitions.

Example: Make sure your baby's world is safe and *secure.*

> **se cure** /pronunciation/ *adj.* **1** protected from danger or harm: *He feels secure in the locked apartment.* **2** not able to be opened or broken, closed tightly: *The jail was secure, with iron bars and a high fence.* **3** sure, confident: *She is secure in knowing that her parents love her.*
> —*v* [T] **-cured, -curing, cures 1** to obtain: *Chin-peng secured a job with a Taiwanese company in New York.* **2** to make a building or area safe: *He secured the office before leaving it for the night.*

The word *secure* can be an adjective and a verb. From the sentence, you know that secure is an adjective that describes "baby's world." Now you must choose which definition of secure as an adjective is correct for this sentence. Try reading each definition as a replacement for *secure* in the sentence. Definition 3 gives a meaning related to the ideas in the reading, but you would not describe a baby's world as sure and confident. Only a person can be sure and confident. However, you might describe a baby's world as protected from danger or harm, so definition 1 is the correct meaning for *secure* in this context.

Practice This Strategy

Read the definitions for the word <u>slow</u> *and decide which definition is used in each sentence.*

> slow /pronunciation/ *adj.* -er, -est **1** not moving fast, moving at a low speed: *The traffic is very slow today.* **2** not smart: *Repeat the directions; he is a bit slow.* **3** not busy or active: *During the summer season, sales are slow for us.* **4** behind the correct time: *My watch is slow; it says 3:00, but the time is 3:15.*
> —*v* **1** [I;T] to go less quickly, lessen speed: *Work has slowed this week, so we can go home earlier.* **2** *phrasal v. sep* [T] to slow something down: *I put on the brakes and slowed the car down.*

Read each sentence and decide if the word <u>slow</u> *is an adjective or a verb. Then write the number of the definition used in the sentence.*

1. Stress can *slow* brain development.
   adjective   verb   definition no. ____

2. This class is too difficult for *slow* learners.
   adjective   verb   definition no. ____

3. Traveling by train is *slower* than traveling by plane.
   adjective   verb   definition no. ____

4. It is not easy to *slow* the bike down if you are going down a hill.
   adjective   verb   definition no. ____

5. Tourism is *slow* during the cold months of the year.
   adjective   verb   definition no. ____

6. If the bus driver's watch is *slow*, the bus may be late.
   adjective   verb   definition no. ____

<u>Remember</u>: Use the context of an unfamiliar word to determine which dictionary definition is appropriate.

You will need to use both context clues and your dictionary to complete your vocabulary journal. After each reading, in Step 2: Read for New Words, you will be prompted to apply these strategies as you complete these steps in your vocabulary journal:

1. Write the word and the sentence in the reading containing the word.

2. Note what part of speech the word should be based on its place in the sentence.

3. Guess the meaning of the word based on the sentence's meaning and the main idea of the reading selection.

4. Discuss your guess with your instructor and classmates, and confirm your guess by looking up the word in the dictionary. Add any notes that will help you remember the meaning of the word.

5. Use the word in your own original sentence.

6. Gloss the reading selection before reading it a second time.

Examples from a Student's Vocabulary Journal

role (n)   *Together with good cleaning habits and practices, these products play an important role in helping to prevent germs from spreading.*
(sentence from reading selection)

Guess: *part, job*

Check: *way in which someone or something is involved in an activity or situation*
(dictionary definition)

Sentence: *Doctors have an important role in helping people stay well.*
(student's practice sentence)

guarantee (v) *According to the Federal Trade Commission, unscrupulous companies guarantee or promise scholarships, grants, or fantastic financial aid packages.*
(sentence from reading selection)

Guess: *promise*

Check: *to promise that something will certainly happen or be*
(dictionary definition)

Sentence: *The college guaranteed a scholarship if I get high grades.*
(student's practice sentence)

generation (n) *Does this mean that today's students are more dishonest than earlier <u>generations</u>?*
(sentence from reading selection)

Guess: *group of people*

Check: *a group of people born and living at about the same time*
(dictionary definition)

Sentence: *The older generation and younger generation often do not enjoy the same kind of music and clothes.*
(student's practice sentence)

Appendix B:
Sample Student Annotations

Confessions of an ESL Teacher

marginalia

I confess. I am a logophile. That means I am a word lover. The words above are from my word collection. I am a <u>compulsive</u> word collector. With all my hundreds of words, I must be a terrific ESL teacher.

Of course, word collecting is a good hobby for an ESL teacher, but there are other advantages.

<u>First, word collecting</u> is a very cheap <u>hobby</u>. Words are everywhere, and the collecting process requires only paper, pencil, and a dictionary. My words <u>reside</u> in special little note-books. Sometimes a word finds a home on a yellow sticky note, on the blank inside pages of books, or in the margins of the text. <u>Housing</u> my collection requires none of the fancy or expensive equipment other collections require.

<u>Second</u>, I get to decide what is collectible. I get to make decisions about which words are <u>worth</u> saving. I am attracted to some words because they are fun to say. Other words, such as *disambiguate*, have the perfect meaning for a thought or feeling that I was sure could not ever be described. *Disambiguate* is a verb, but it's not in the dictionary. It means to make something clear. It was formed from the adjective, *ambiguous*, which describes something that is unclear or confusing. *Disambiguate* was <u>coined</u> (<u>made up</u>) by the Pentagon, the

<u>hobby</u> = hobi
something to do
for fun, not work

<u>housing</u>
provide a place to
someone or something

<u>worth</u>
something having
a value in money

<u>disambiguate</u>
(*inventado por el peuta
gono*) make clear
Telling to someone to
make clear with some
thing

<u>coined</u>
invent a new word that
everybody began to use

175

marginalia

military department of the U.S. government. I bet a lot of ESL students want their teacher to disambiguate English grammar. Another one of my favorite words is *caveat*. It is on my list because I simply cannot remember its meaning. I have finally given in, and I have <u>dog-eared</u> that page of one of my dictionaries. These are only a few of the reasons for my word choices.

<u>dog-ear(ed)</u>
turn down corner
of a page
easy to find

professional = *meslek*
   adj   *job*

Finally, the most important advantage is a <u>professional</u> one. Shouldn't a logophile make a good ESL teacher? Word collecting is the perfect hobby for an ESL teacher. But here is my most embarrassing confession: *I really do not know how to teach vocabulary.* Maybe I can help students find ways to study new words, but really teach? I am guilty of having students <u>match</u> words and meanings, write definitions, identify related words, write sentences, fill in blanks, take words apart and put them back together, play word games, discuss meanings and uses, and countless other activities. Now, this list of activities makes me laugh. Even funnier is my final confession: I have forgotten the meanings of *many of the words* on the opening list just like many A+ students who have forgotten word meanings after a test. How can this be possible?

<u>match</u>
two things that have
resource style or
pattern or color

I can only conclude that there must be many secrets to second language vocabulary learning. In this chapter, you will begin working on unfamiliar words, and most important, the activities that depend on words—reading and writing. Maybe, you can solve the mystery of learning second language vocabulary.

Based on your first reading, complete this outline:

The topic: <u>*Vocabulary*</u>

The main idea: <u>*There are advantages to collecting words especially for an ESL teacher.*</u>

                             <u>*Collecting words is the one of the best ways to learn new words.*</u>

Some supporting ideas: <u>*collecting words*</u>

Step 1: Read for the Main Idea

First, read the selection quickly. Read it from beginning to end, and try to understand the writer's main idea and a few supporting ideas. Notice that some AWL words for vocabulary study are underlined. Underline any other words that are unfamiliar to you. Don't stop reading to look them up. Complete the outline at the end of the selection.

Reading Well

To read well, readers must be <u>active</u>—never passive. Reading may seem like a passive activity, but it requires serious attention in order to understand a writer's message. The same kind of interaction that connects speaker and listener must occur between writer and reader, but with one big difference— the writer has only one chance to offer his ideas and thoughts. However, the reader has many chances to understand them. The reader can return to a reading selection again and again. *Active reading requires revision* or changes in the same way that writing requires revision. Like the first copy or <u>draft</u> of a composition, the first reading is only a starting <u>place</u>.

As an academic reader, you must find ways to understand the writer's message. After your first quick nonstop reading, it's time to dig deeper into the reading selection.

This is where the action starts. Throw away your favorite yellow <u>highlighter</u>. (I know this sounds a little crazy.) It is a passive learning tool. It's too easy to read and mark and mark and mark and mark. Before long, you've got a page that's mostly yellow, right? To read with real understanding, you must become <u>*involved*</u> with the writer. Successful academic readers read with a pencil in hand. They are ready to respond and question the writer. They write notes in the margins of their reading selections. Such notes are called *margin annotations* or *marginalia*. These are brief comments, questions, reactions, drawings, stars, or anything that is helpful. School-teachers know this habit as "book abuse" because it shouldn't

marginalia
readers must be active

writer /opport give
idea reader sev. opport
underst

active reading & writing
req revision

draft
a group of ideas
For the final person

point n place

highlighter
a pen to mark words
in color

Things I can write

be done in books you don't own. Librarians think of themselves as the "book police" and fine people who write margin
notes for their crimes. Good students (who have their own
books) know this as a valuable learning strategy.

marginala

strategy
way to do something

Marginalia are personalized tools, so you do not have to
write in a way that others can read and understand. You are
creating a personal learning tool.

personalized -
only for me

creating - making

The margins are a good place for:

- questioning the writer's views and sources
- agreeing or disagreeing with the writer
- marking key concepts to remember
- marking key concepts to clarify
- marking ideas to use in writing or discussion
- drawing connections to other information you have
  or other things you've read

concepts are ideas

Look at the examples of marginalia in Appendix B. What
kinds of things are marked in this student example?

Steps 3–5 of the reading selections require careful reading
and rereading. Add marginalia as you do your careful reading.
Continue to go through the reading selection, trying to understand more each time you read it. Your annotated text will be
useful for class discussions, so mark any parts that you need
to ask about during class discussions.

require
need
have to do

? for class

This is the way successful academic readers read after they
have discovered the main idea. Remember: The more involved
you are with the writer, the more you will understand and
remember. Then you will have more to say in your writing.

I'm talking to the writer.

Use in my writing

Step 1: Read for the Main Ideas

First, read the selection quickly. Read it from beginning to end, and try to understand the writer's main idea and a few supporting ideas. Note that some AWL words for vocabulary study are underlined. Underline any other words that are unfamiliar to you. Don't stop reading to look them up. Complete the outline at the end of the selection.

Writing in Circles

marginalia

As a college student, you will have to show your understanding of various subjects by writing. The writing work in this book will help prepare you for this task.

Many first and second language writing teachers teach writing as a process that can be divided into separate steps: pre-writing, drafting, revising, and editing. Each step has a purpose.

teach writing in separate steps

Step	Purpose
pre-writing	to choose a topic, <u>gather</u> and <u>sort</u> ideas, and decide the treatment of the topic
drafting	to write your ideas
revising	to evaluate your written ideas and improve them
editing	to correct mechanical errors (usage, grammar, spelling, etc.)

gather
collect something, put together, accumulate

sort
classify or separate something

Writers move from one step to the next. They complete each step before moving to the next step. This is referred to as a *linear writing process*. Many writers like the feeling of organization that comes from working through the steps.

linear writing process
move one step to the next
This way many writers

Other writers switch back and <u>forth</u> between the steps. This is referred to as *recursive writing process*. This style of writing is more like the way many people think. There are always thoughts entering our minds.

forth
forward - go straight ahead

In <u>recursive</u> writing, the same steps of writing are used, but they are *not always used in linear order*. The writing process is considered nonlinear. In other words, you don't have to complete one step before moving on to the next, and you can

recursive writing process
switch back and forth between the steps

This way many people

marginalia

return to any step at any time. You might do some revising or editing while you are still drafting. You might add an idea that was not in your prewriting. You might even return to a reading selection or your writing journal. It's even OK to change your topic sentence.

Many writers are more comfortable with recursive writing. Lots of writers use a recursive writing method without even knowing it. Recursive writers know that revising is the key to saying what they mean. Remember Susan Sontag's quote? "Then comes the warm part: when you already have something to work with, upgrade, edit." As a novice second language writer, practice the recursive method of writing. Go back and forth between writing steps; do all of those re- activities—*reread, revise, rewrite, return to a classmate for discussion,* and *resubmit* your drafts to your teacher. The writing tasks in this text will help you discover the rewards of the recursive writing process. Remember, a better process <u>yields</u> a better product.

<u>this writer say</u>
RW is better than other method

?

<u>RW know revisions</u>
is the key to say what they mean

<u>resubmit</u>
Recheck from authority

<u>yields</u> =
render
produce
give us return

Based on your first reading of the selection, complete this outline.

The topic: <u>(How to write) writing</u>

The main idea: <u>The best way to write</u>

- <u>There are 2 different kinds of writing processes.</u>

- <u>R & L writing process are two = ways think about writing.</u>

- <u>Some students find recursive writing easier than linear writing.</u>

Index of Vocabulary from the Academic Word List

This list includes all of the AWL (Coxhead 2000) words included in the text by chapter and reading, excluding duplicates. Words in bold are included in Step 2: Read for New Words.

CHAPTER 1
ambiguous 1-1
chapter 1-1
conclude 1-1
definitions 1-1
equipment 1-1
final 1-1
finally 1-1
identify 1-1
margins 1-1
military 1-1
process1-1
professional 1-1
require 1-1
reside 1-1
text 1-1
academic 1-2
brief 1-2
clarify 1-2
comments 1-2
concept 1-2
creating 1-2
draft 1-2
interaction 1-2
involved 1-2

margin 1-2
margins 1-2
occur 1-2
passive 1-2
reactions 1-2
require 1-2
requires 1-2
respond 1-2
revision 1-2
selection 1-2
selections 1-2
sources 1-2
strategy 1-2
text 1-2
draft 1-3
drafting 1-3
drafts 1-3
edit 1-3
editing 1-3
errors 1-3
evaluate 1-3
journal 1-3
process 1-3
quote 1-3
revise 1-3

revising 1-3
selection 1-3
style 1-3
task 1-3
text 1-3
topic 1-3

CHAPTER 2
consumers 2-1
environment 2-1
evaluate 2-1
evidence 2-1
involved 2-1
labeled 2-1
medical 2-1
normal 2-1
overall 2-1
primary 2-1
professionals 2-1
research 2-1
researcher 2-1
survey 2-1
survive 2-1
chart 2-2
concentration 2-2

consumer 2-2
contact 2-2
eliminate 2-2
formulation 2-2
generated 2-2
inhibit 2-2
initially 2-2
period 2-2
removes 2-2
role 2-2
section 2-2
significantly 2-2
transmitted 2-2

CHAPTER 3
access 3-1
aid 3-1
attach 3-1
behalf 3-1
commission 3-1
confirm 3-1
consent 3-1
creative 3-1
credit 3-1
despite 3-1
federal 3-1
fee 3-1
finance 3-1
financial 3-1
foundation 3-1
grants 3-1
guarantee 3-1
guaranteed 3-1
investigate 3-1
policies 3-1
policy 3-1
potential 3-1
purchasing 3-1
quote 3-1

reluctant 3-1
require 3-1
required 3-1
selected 3-1
academic 3-2
adults 3-2
attitude 3-2
attitudes 3-2
code 3-3
communication 3-2
conduct 3-2
consequences 3-2
devices 3-2
display 3-2
eliminate 3-2
eliminating 3-2
ethics 3-2
finances 3-2
formulas 3-2
generation 3-2
grading 3-2
identify 3-2
indicates 3-2
individual 3-2
institute 3-2
instructors 3-2
integrity 3-2
involvement 3-2
involves 3-2
methods 3-2
occurred 3-2
phenomenon 3-2
promote 3-2
promoting 3-2
remove 3-2
research 3-2
researchers 3-2
sources 3-2
survey 3-2

task 3-2
technology 3-2
varied 3-2

CHAPTER 4
adjusted 4-1
adults 4-1
appropriate 4-1
bond 4-1
communities 4-1
complex 4-1
consistently 4-1
ensure 4-1
environment 4-1
finally 4-1
function 4-1
functions 4-1
furthermore 4-1
interact 4-1
interacting 4-1
positive 4-1
process 4-1
regulate 4-1
remove 4-1
respond 4-1
role 4-1
secure 4-1
similar 4-1
stress 4-1
survive 4-1
adult 4-2
contributed 4-2
decade 4-2
media 4-2
notion 4-2
occupational 4-2
physical 4-2
published 4-2
researcher 4-2
response 4-2

CHAPTER 5
achieved 5-1
adults 5-1
annually 5-1
authority 5-1
capacity 5-1
cent 5-1
communication 5-1
construction 5-1
creative 5-1
credit 5-1
culture 5-1
define 5-1
design 5-1
emphasize 5-1
energetic 5-1
energy 5-1
equipped 5-1
evaluation 5-1
evaluations 5-1
facility 5-1
founder 5-1
founders 5-1
furthermore 5-1
goals 5-1
individual 5-1
innovation 5-1
institute 5-1
items 5-1
job 5-1
labor 5-1
license 5-1
located 5-1
maintenance 5-1
medium 5-1
orientation 5-1
participate 5-1
participation 5-1
partners 5-1
policy 5-1
process 5-1

professionals 5-1
registered 5-1
resource 5-1
resources 5-1
revolutionary 5-1
team 5-1
technical 5-1
technology 5-1
traditional 5-1
area 5-2
assigned 5-2
available 5-2
created 5-2
eventually 5-2
finally 5-2
financial 5-2
goal 5-2
issue 5-2
percent 5-2
revenues 5-2
statistics 5-2
survey 5-2
transportation 5-2

CHAPTER 6
assume 6-1
author 6-1
chapter 6-1
chemical 6-1
created 6-1
creating 6-1
creator 6-1
eventually 6-1
evolution 6-1
evolutionist 6-1
instance 6-1
occur 6-1
persists 6-1
process 6-1
reaction 6-1
responds 6-1

selection 6-1
theory 6-1
undergo 6-1
benefits 6-2
community 6-2
emphasizes 6-2
environmentalists 6-2
ethics 6-2
responded 6-2
technology 6-2
traditions 6-2

CHAPTER 7
abnormal 7-1
adults 7-1
alterations 7-1
approach 7-1
benefits 7-1
challenged 7-1
consultant 7-1
controversial 7-1
controversies 7-1
create 7-1
creation 7-1
design 7-1
discriminated 7-1
diversity 7-1
economics 7-1
eliminated 7-1
emphasis 7-1
ethical 7-1
ethics 7-1
excluded 7-1
expert 7-1
impact 7-1
impacted 7-1
individual 7-1
interact 7-1
issues 7-1
medical 7-1
occurred 7-1

predictions 7-1
professionals 7-1
project 7-1
registered 7-1
research 7-1
researcher 7-1
resolution 7-1
respond 7-1
structure 7-1
technology 7-1
termination 7-1
violated 7-1
volunteer 7-1
abnormal 7-2
areas 7-2
available 7-2

challenges 7-2
consequence 7-2
constitution 7-2
contract 7-2
contracted 7-2
deny 7-2
dramatic 7-2
eliminate 7-2
enable 7-2
energy 7-2
environmental 7-2
finally 7-2
fundamental 7-2
furthermore 7-2
identification 7-2
identified 7-2

identity 7-2
impact 7-2
individual 7-2
individuals 7-2
medical 7-2
normal 7-2
potential 7-2
prediction 7-2
predictions 7-2
project 7-2
revolutionize 7-2
sequence 7-2
technology 7-2

CHAPTER 8
finally 8-1